Chinese for Beginners
A Comprehensive Guide for Learning the Chinese Language Quickly

© Copyright 2020

All Rights Reserved. No part of this book may be reproduced in any form without permission in writing from the author. Reviewers may quote brief passages in reviews.

Disclaimer: No part of this publication may be reproduced or transmitted in any form or by any means, mechanical or electronic, including photocopying or recording, or by any information storage and retrieval system, or transmitted by email without permission in writing from the publisher.

While all attempts have been made to verify the information provided in this publication, neither the author nor the publisher assumes any responsibility for errors, omissions or contrary interpretations of the subject matter herein.

This book is for entertainment purposes only. The views expressed are those of the author alone, and should not be taken as expert instruction or commands. The reader is responsible for his or her own actions.

Adherence to all applicable laws and regulations, including international, federal, state and local laws governing professional licensing, business practices, advertising and all other aspects of doing business in the US, Canada, UK or any other jurisdiction is the sole responsibility of the purchaser or reader.

Neither the author nor the publisher assumes any responsibility or liability whatsoever on the behalf of the purchaser or reader of these materials. Any perceived slight of any individual or organization is purely unintentional.

Contents

INTRODUCTION 1
PART ONE: THE VERY BASICS 4
CHAPTER 1: THE CHINESE ALPHABET 5
CHAPTER 2: NOUNS, PRONOUNS, AND ADJECTIVES 12
CHAPTER 3: VERBS AND AUXILIARY VERBS 19
CHAPTER 4: NUMERALS AND MEASURE WORDS 25
CHAPTER 5: AUXILIARY WORDS 32
PART TWO: GRAMMAR 38
CHAPTER 6: PHRASES AND SENTENCE ELEMENTS 39
CHAPTER 7: SIMPLE AND COMPLEX SENTENCES 48
PART THREE: CONVERSATION 53
CHAPTER 8: BASIC GREETINGS 55
CHAPTER 9: INTRODUCING YOURSELF 58
CHAPTER 10: FORMULATING QUESTIONS AND DIALOGUE: 67
APPENDIX: VOCABULARY 85
GLOSSARY OF NOUNS 85

Introduction

The Chinese language (or group of related languages) is spoken by the Han, who constitute 94% of China's population. One word for the language in Chinese is 汉语 (hàn yǔ). The Chinese language is divided into several major dialects (with many sub-dialects). Speakers of different dialects can in some cases find each other unintelligible, but are brought together by the fact that they share a common script.

Chinese for Beginners describes the primary and official dialect, which is known by many names: Mandarin, Modern Standard Chinese, or *Putonghua* (common speech). This is a practical textbook designed for foreigners who are interested in learning Chinese through self-study and help them effectively master basic Chinese communication skulls within a short period of time.

In the last 20 years, more and more people from different parts of the world have come to China. Everybody experiences their own story and is often shocked by the changes in this fast-growing country. For expats living in China, many want and need to learn Mandarin Chinese. However, due to work commitments during the day and family activities after hours, it is sometimes difficult find the time to attend full-time language classes.

As professional language instructors with years of experience in corporate Chinese training, we have found that most language learning textbooks are designed for full-time training over a long term. It has been very difficult to find a practical book to help people start communicating as soon as possible. Therefore, we made up our mind and wrote the book *Chinese for Beginners* in 2020.

To make sure that the content is both practical and fun, we chose vocabulary based on the *HSK Guideline for Chinese Words and Characters*. We also used many words and dialogues that concern Chinese society as well as a foreigner's daily life, study, and work in China. In terms of grammar, we made explicit and practical examples to help users apply these points in a flexible manner. Language points are arranged from easiest to hardest and simplest forms to most complicated. Explanations present material in a way which meets the needs of students and is easy to learn.

Focusing on conversation, *Chinese for Beginners* was designed for those who can only read the book several times a week. The full book can be finished in a month. In order to help different types of readers find what they want to improve through this book, we have divided the book into four parts:

Part one begins with proper pronunciation in Mandarin. Readers using this book will get thorough training in phonetics. We introduce, explain, and emphasize points that are typical in Chinese phonetics and particularly difficult for beginners to grasp. Readers will learn numbers, months, and days of the week. After basic knowledge of articles, nouns, pronouns, prepositions, and adjectives is introduced.

Part two introduces basic Chinese grammar, including some special Chinese sentence structures which are very popular in daily oral Chinese. Since language is such an important aspect of Chinese culture, we also introduce elements of politeness to help learners to deal with common social situations.

Part three covers a wide range of typical situations in a students' daily social life including "Basic Greetings", "Introducing Yourself", "Buying and Ordering", "At Work", "At School/College", "Travelling", "Socializing", "Formal Events", and other common encounters. The language used is natural, standard, and vivid. Attention has been given to introducing aspects of

Chinese culture while maintaining a level suitable for beginners. In these ways, the basic material is covered thoroughly while things are kept interesting.

Finally, we have an appendix to introduce you more nouns and verbs. All words are written in characters and phonetic transcriptions in the *pinyin* system with their speech portions and English equivalents provided. In order to provide students with a more exact understanding of the meanings and the usages of words. Some words are also accompanied with explanations rather than just English equivalents. Nevertheless, students should not expect to learn the meaning and usage of word by depending only on the English translation, which will often hold true only for a particular context.

Chinese for Beginners is also a good choice for people who would like to take an intensive course before going to China for business or pleasure.

Learning basic Chinese is not as difficult as you may think at first. Even the simplest knowledge of the language will enhance your experience. Our wish is to help you enjoy your life in China. We sincerely hope that learners may benefit from *Chinese for Beginners* and achieve more progress in the future. We firmly believe that more and more friends will come to China and start learning this ancient language. Good luck!

PART ONE: THE VERY BASICS

Chapter 1: The Chinese Alphabet

Everybody knows that Chinese is a kind of pictographic language. Each word is made of characters. Each character is monosyllabic and has its own pronunciation. Chinese people mark the pronunciation of characters in pinyin (Chinese phonetic alphabets). There are two groups of alphabets in pinyin. One group is used at the beginning of a syllable and is called initials. The other group follows initials that are called finals.
There are 23 initials in modern Chinese:
b-, p-, m-, f-, d-, t-, n-, l-, g-, k-, h-, j-, q-, x-, z-, c-, s-, r-, zh-, ch-, sh-, y-, w-
The final with only one vowel is called a simple final. There are six of them:
-a, -o, -e, -i, -u, -ü
Finals made up of two or three vowels are called compound finals. There are 13 of them:
-ai, -ao, -ou, -ei, -ia, -ie, -iao, -ua, -uo, -uai, -üe, -iu, -ui
Finals with nasal endings are finals followed by –n or –ng. There are 16 of them:
-an, -ang, -ong, -en, -eng, -in, -ing, -ian, -iang, -iong, -eng, -un, -uan, -uang, -ün, -üan

Potential Trouble Spots
1. For a completed syllable, finals including i, u, or ü and finals starting with one of them should follow an initial. Finals that include a, o, or e and finals that start with one of them can be an independent syllable.
2. When -ü, -üe, -üan, and -ün follow j-, q-, x-, or y-, the two dots on the top of them are dropped. As such, it is yue and not yüe; yuan and not yüan. In addition, j-, q-, and x- can only combine with finals that start with -i and –ü.
3. The retroflex sounds: zh-, ch-, sh-, and r-. These initials are called retroflex sounds because they are all pronounced with the tongue curved back into the middle of mouth. For the first three of these, there is a corresponding sound that is pronounced further forward in the mouth, and one key to mastering standard Chinese pronunciation is being able to distinguish between the retroflex initial and its more forward counterpart. The pairs are:
zh- and j-. Both sound something like the "j" in "jump", but for zh-, the tip of the tongue is a little further back and for j- it is further forward.
ch- and q-. Both are like the "ch" in "chip", but for ch-, the tongue is further back and for q- it is further forward.
sh- and x-. Both are like the "sh" in "ship", but for sh-, the tongue is further back and for x-, it is further forward.
Retroflex sounds are more typical of northern Chinese speech than that of other parts of China; in fact, in many parts of China, people pronounce all these sounds with their tongue forward. zh- thus becomes z-, ch- becomes c-, and sh- becomes s-. While you should try to pronounce them in a standard manner, your ears need to get used to the many Chinese speakers who don't make these distinctions. You may also take comfort in the fact that many Chinese find the distinction between these pairs as troublesome as you may.
One way the sounds above are distinguished from each other is by the position of the tongue. They are also distinguished as much or

more by the fact that j-, q-, and x- are always followed by a high front vowel, either –i or –ü, while zh-, ch-, and sh- never are. As such, even if you pronounce both members of a pair the same way, there is little probability of confusion as long as you get the rest of the word right.

4. In addition to the retroflex sounds discussed above, there are a few other sounds in Chinese that are just plain difficult for English speakers to make.

Chief amongst the trouble makers is the initial retroflex sound r-. It is pronounced like the "r" in "rank", but with the tongue just a bit higher so that is buzzes ever so slightly. Again, in many parts of China, people don't make this sound in a way that would pass for standard in Beijing, so you will be allowed some latitude in getting this one right.

 The next one is c-. This "ts" sound does exist in English but is never present in the beginning of words. To make it, first say "cats" and then eliminate the "ca-" part.

English does not have the –ü sound. The simplest explanation is that it is a combination of "ooo" and "eee". To make it, make an "eee" sound with your jaw, and then round your lips for an "ooo" without moving your jaw.

5. On a whole, the *Pinyin* system is quite logical, though there are a few anomalies that may trip you up of you are not careful.

The -i. Usually this is pronounced like "ee" as in "he". But after the c-, s-, z-, ch-, sh-, zh-, or r-, it is pronounced as a short vowel, similar to the "i" in "it". The easiest way to cope with this is just to memorize that the following spellings require the short sound: ci, si, zi, zhi, chi, shi, and ri.

The -e. When alone, this is pronounced like "uh" in English, similar to the "u" in "under". In the following combinations, it is pronounced as follows:

The -ie sounds like the "ye" in "yes".

The -ue like the "we" in "wet".

The ye, again, sounds like the "ye" in "yes".

The –ian. Despite the "a", this sound is pronounced like the word "yen". Moreover, yan is also pronounced as "yen".

The -ui. This is pronounced like "way". We might expect this sound to be spelled as –uei, but no such luck. At least it isn't spelled "weigh".

Tones

Among the components of a Chinese syllable, there is also a tone besides the initial and the final. Altogether, there are four tones:

The first tone (the high tone)

The second tone (the rising tone)

The third tone (the falling-rising tone)

The fourth tone (the falling tone)

Syllables with same initials and finals in different tones usually have different meanings. For example:

tū, the Chinese character 秃, which means to be bold.

tú, the Chinese character 图, which means a map or a painting

tǔ, the Chinese character 土, which means earth or soil.

tù, the Chinese character 兔, which means a rabbit.

If a syllable preceded by another one is not stressed, it loses its tonal value and becomes short and weak. We call this the neutral tone, for example:

姐姐（jiě jie）older sister

孩子（hái zi）child

便宜（pián yi）cheap

In modern Chinese, there is a special grammatical phenomenon called tone-sandi.

When two 3rd tones are next to each other, the first one changes into a 2nd tone.

手表（shǒu biǎo）wrist watch

你好（nǐ hǎo）hello

很冷（hěn lěng）very cold

When 一 is placed before a syllable carrying the 4th tone, it is read in the 2nd tone (yí). When placed before a syllable carrying the 1st tone, the 2nd tone or the 3rd tone, it is read in the 4th tone (yì). When it is read independently or at the end of a word, 一 is pronounced as its original tone (yī).

"不" is pronounced in the 2nd tone (bú) when it precedes a 4th tone syllable. The tone of 不 does not change when it stands by itself or precedes a 1st, 2nd or a 3rd tone, pronounced (bù).

Exercise

1. Make a distinction between these difficult sounds:

b- and p-
辫子（biàn zi）pigtail
骗子（piàn zi）liar

d- and t-
读书（dú shū）reading
图书（tú shū）books

g- and k-
天宫（tiān gōng）heavenly palace
天空（tiān kōng）sky

zh- and ch-
竹子（zhú zi）bamboo
厨子（chú zi）cook

j- and q-
捐钱（juān qián）to denote
圈钱（quān qián）to collect money illegally

q- and x-
情形（qíng xíng）condition, situation, circumstances
行刑（xíng xíng）to execute

j- and x-
聚集（jù jí）to gather
续集（xù jí）sequel

s- and sh-
散开（sǎn kāi）to scatter

闪开（shǎn kāi）to get out of the way

c- and s-

一次（yí cì）one time

疑似（yí sì）seemingly certain but at the same time uncertain

z- and c-

没做（méi zuò）didn't do something

没错（méi cuò）didn't go wrong

-an and -en

瞻仰（zhān yǎng）to look at with reverence

真痒（zhēn yǎng）really itchy

-ang and -eng

东方（dōng fāng）east

东风（dōng fēng）east wind

-an and -ang

山口（shān kǒu）mountain pass

伤口（shāng kǒu）wound

-en and -eng

渗水（shèn shuǐ）to leak water

圣水（shèng shuǐ）holy water

2. Make a distinction between these different tones:

奴隶（nú lì）slave

努力（nǔ lì）to make great efforts

同班（tóng bān）classmate

同伴（tóng bàn）companion

仔细（zǐ xì）careful

自习（zì xí）self-study

松树（sōng shù）pine tree

松鼠（sōng shǔ）squirrel

徽章（huī zhāng）badge

会长（huì zhǎng）president of an association

孤立（gū lì）to isolate

鼓励（gǔ lì）to encourage
重视（zhòng shì）to attach importance to
忠实（zhōng shí）faithful
真鲜（zhēn xiān）really tasty
真咸（zhēn xián）really salty
真险（zhēn xiǎn）really dangerous
针线（zhēn xiàn）sewing
争执（zhēng zhí）dispute
整治（zhěng zhì）to fix or repair
正直（zhèng zhí）honest
政治（zhèng zhì）politics

3. Read the following words and pay attention to the neutral tones:
妈妈（mā ma）mother
回来（huí lai）to come back
办法（bàn fa）idea, method
东西（dōng xi）thing
棉花（mián hua）cotton
帽子（mào zi）hat, cap

4. Read the following words and pay attention to tone-sandhi
舞蹈（wǔ dǎo）dance
女友（nǔ yǒu）girlfriend
影响（yǐng xiǎng）influence
引导（yǐn dǎo）guidance
表演（biǎo yǎn）to act
野草（yě cǎo）weeds

Chapter 2: Nouns, Pronouns, and Adjectives

Nouns

A word denoting the name of a person or a thing is called a noun. Nouns in Chinese are not specifically identified as being nouns except in the case of those with suffixes such as 子 (zi), 儿 (er), 头 (tóu), etc. Generally, a noun can be preceded by a numeral and measure word combination but cannot be modified by adverbs.

Nouns can be assigned to different categories with reference to their grammatical properties. In general, we have common nouns, abstract nouns, and proper nouns.

Chinese nouns do not under any circumstances inflect for case, gender, or number. Therefore, in a language without definite or indefinite articles like Chinese, the reference of unmarked nouns is influenced by a number of factors: context, sentence type, the position of the noun in relation to the verb in the sentence, and the nature of the verb itself. When we use the noun 书 (shū) book, for instance, we have no way of determining whether it means "the book" or "books" in general until we place it in a sentence.

There are a group of nouns that have an inbuilt notion of plurality. For example:

父母（fù mǔ）parents

夫妻（fū qī）a married couple

子女（zǐ nǚ）children

师生（shī shēng）teachers and students

亲友（qīn yǒu）friends and relatives

财产（cái chǎn）possessions

树木（shù mù）trees

文具（wén jù）stationery

车辆（chē liàng）vehicles

花朵（huā duǒ）flowers

马匹（mǎ pǐ）horses

纸张（zhǐ zhāng）paper

砖块（zhuān kuài）bricks

Note that the last five examples above are formed by tagging measure words (辆、朵、匹、张、块) to nouns (车、花、马、纸、砖). If we put numerals and measure words in front of the nouns, they will still make sense.

一辆车（yí liàng chē）a car

两朵花（liǎng duǒ huā）two flowers

三匹马（sān pǐ mǎ）three horses

四张纸（sì zhāng zhǐ）four pieces of paper

五块砖（wǔ kuài zhuān）five bricks

The suffix 们 (men) can be added to a personal noun to express a plural. For example, 老师们 (lǎo shī men) means "teachers". However, if there are numeral measure words or other words implying the plural before the noun, the suffix 们 (men) can't be added to the noun. For example, we can't say 五个学生们 (wǔ gè xué shēng men), and should say 五个学生 (wǔ gè xué shēng) instead.

Generally, a noun can serve as a subject, object, attributive, or predicate in a sentence. Let's read some examples one by one.

1. As a subject:

北京是中国的首都（běi jīng shì zhōng guó de shǒu dū）。
Beijing is the capital of China.

冬天冷，夏天热（dōng tiān lěng, xià tiān rè）。
In winter it is cold; in summer it is hot.

东边是操场（dōng biān shì cāo chǎng）。
The playground is to the east.

教授给我们上课（jiào shòu gěi wǒ men shàng kè）。
The professor taught us a course.

2. As an object:

彼得正在看书（bǐ dé zhèng zài kàn shū）。
Peter is reading books.

现在五点了 (xiàn zài wǔ diǎn le)。
It is now five o'clock.

我家在北边 (wǒ jiā zài běi biān)。
My house is to the north.

她不想写作业 (tā bù xiǎng xiě zuò yè)。
She doesn't want to do her homework.

3. As an attributive with or without 的 (de) indicating attribution or possession:

我喜欢秋天的夜晚 (wǒ xǐ huān qiū tiān de yè wǎn)。
I like the night in autumn.

中文语法并不难 (zhōng wén yǔ fǎ bìng bù nán)。
Chinese grammar is not difficult.

这是德国产品 (zhè shì dé guó chǎn pǐn)。
This is a product from Germany.

4. As a predicate:

今天晴天（jīn tiān qíng tiān）。

Today is a sunny day.
昨天周一（zuó tiān zhōu yī）。
Yesterday was Monday.

5. Time nouns (indicating date, times, seasons, etc) and nouns of locality (those showing the direction to a location) can also serve as adverbial adjuncts, whereas nouns of other kinds cannot. For example:

他后天来（tā hòu tiān lái）。
He will arrive the day after tomorrow.

我们晚上上课（wǒ men wǎn shàng shàng kè）。
We have classes in the evening.

您这边请（nín zhè biān qǐng）。
This way please.

请外边抽烟（qǐng wài biān chōu yān）。
Please smoke outside.

Pronouns

Pronouns are the words that stand for nouns, verbs, adjectives, numerals, and adverbs. Chinese pronouns are classified as:

1. A pronoun which refers to persons or things is called a personal pronoun. Personal pronouns cannot be reduplicated, and they cannot take words of other parts of speech as prepositioned modifiers. For example:

我（wǒ）I, me
你（nǐ）you
他（tā）he, him
她（tā）she, her
我们（wǒ men）we, us
你们（nǐ men）you
咱们（zán men）we, us

2. A pronoun which is used to distinguish people or things is called a demonstrative pronoun. For example:

这（zhè）here

那（nà）there

3. A pronoun which is used to indicate interrogation is called an interrogative pronoun. For example:

谁（shuí）who, whom

什么（shén me）what

哪里（nǎ lǐ）where

多少（duō shǎo）how much

怎么（zěn me）how

Pronouns serve basically the same function as the words which they subsitute. Therefore, a pronoun can serve as a subject, object, attributive, adverbial adjunct, predicate, or a complement.

Adjectives

Words that describe the shape or property of a person or thing, the state of a movement, or action are called adjectives. Most adjectives can be modified by adverbs of degree. The negative adverb 不 (bù) is placed before an adjective to achieve their negative form.

Adjectives include the following kinds:

1. Describing shape, for example:

大（dà）big, large, wide, old

小（xiǎo）small, young

高（gāo）tall

矮（ǎi）short 美丽（měi lì）beautiful

帅（shuài）handsome

2. Describing the property of quality, for example:

好（hǎo）good, well

坏（huài）bad, spoiled

冷（lěng）cold

热（rè）hot

对（duì）right

错（cuò）wrong

正确（zhèng què）correct

伟大（wěi dà）great

优秀（yōu xiù）outstanding, excellent

严重（yán zhòng）serious, critical, grave, severe

3. Describing the state of a movement or action, for example:

快（kuài）fast, quick, swift

慢（màn）slow

紧张（jǐn zhāng）nervous

流利（liú lì）fluent

认真（rèn zhēn）earnest, serious

熟练（shú liàn）proficient, skilled

残酷（cán kù）cruel

In Chinese, adjectives have many functions in a sentence. Let's analyze them one by one.

1. Adjectives are mainly used as modifying attributives.

她穿了一件红裙子（tā chuān le yí jiàn hóng qún zi）。

She's wearing a red skirt.

他戴了一顶黑帽子（tā dài le yì dǐng hēi mào zi）。

He's wearing a black hat.

在乡下可以观赏宽广的原野（zài xiāng xià kě yǐ guān shǎng kuān guǎng de yuán yě）。

You can enjoy the vast expanse of the countryside fields.

我喜欢蔚蓝的天空和明媚的阳光（wǒ xǐ huān wèi lán de tiān kōng hé míng mèi de yáng guāng）。

I enjoy the blue sky and bright sunshine.

2. An adjective can serve as a predicate.

我们的时间非常紧迫（wǒ men de shí jiān fēi cháng jǐn pò）。

We have a very tight schedule.

她很漂亮（tā hěn piào liàng）。

She's very pretty.

他很矮（tā hěn ǎi）。

He's short.

百合花很香（bǎi hé huā hěn xiāng）。
Lilys are very fragrant.

3. Another of the important uses of adjectives is placed before a verb as an adverbial adjunct.

她高兴地走了（tā gāo xìng de zǒu le）。
She left happily.

他正在大声地叫喊（tā zhèng zài de shēng dì jiào hǎn）。
He's shouting loudly.

我可以流利地说中文（wǒ kě yǐ liú lì de shuō zhōng wén）。
I can speak Chinese fluently.

4. Adjectives often serve as complements to predicate verbs.

把你的衣服擦干净（bǎ nǐ de yī fu cā gàn jìng）。
Clean your clothes.

风吹干了衣服（fēng chuī gān le yī fu）。
The wind dried the clothes.

5. An adjective can serve as a subject.

谦虚是中国的传统美德（qiān xū shì zhōng guó de chuán tǒng měi dé）。
Modesty is a traditional virtue in Chinese culture.

骄傲使人落后（jiāo ào shǐ rén luò hòu）。
Pride will make you fall behind.

6. An adjective can serve as an object.

我喜欢安静（wǒ xǐ huān ān jìng）。
I like the quiet.

女孩子爱漂亮（nǚ hái zi ài piào liàng）。
Girls love being pretty.

Chapter 3: Verbs and Auxiliary Verbs

Verbs
Words indicating actions, behavior, mental activities, changes and development, etc. are called verbs. Verbs can be grouped into transitive verbs and intransitive verbs according to whether they take an object. Verbs that can be followed immediately by an object are called transitive verbs. Verbs that can't immediately take an object are called intransitive verbs. Verbs can be negated by the negative adverbs 不（bù）, 没（méi）, or 没有（méi yǒu）.

1. As a predicate
我喜欢旅游（wǒ xǐ huān lǚ yóu）。
I like travelling.
她坐在椅子上（tā zuò zài yǐ zi shàng）。
She's sitting on a chair.

2. As a subject
A verb can be used as a subject on the condition that the predicate of the sentence is an adjective or a verb expressing the ideas of "stop, start, or judge".
浪费可耻（làng fèi kě chǐ）。

Waste is disgraceful.
战斗开始了（zhàn dòu kāi shǐ le）。
The fight begins.

3. As an attributive

的（de）must be added to a verb used as an attributive.
你有喝的东西吗（nǐ yǒu hē de dōng xī ma）？
Do you have something to drink?
他说的话很对（tā shuō de huà hěn duì）。
What he said is correct.

4. As an object

我喜欢游泳（wǒ xǐ huān yóu yǒng）。
I like swimming.
他们十一点结束了讨论（tā men shí yī diǎn jié shù le tǎo lùn）。
They ended the discussion at 11 o'clock.

5. As a complement

车开过来了（chē kāi guò lái le）。
The car came over.
我听得懂（wǒ tīng de dǒng）。
I understand.

6. As an adverbial adjunct

Note that only auxiliary verbs can serve as an adverbial adjunct. We will introduce you more about auxiliary verbs in the next chapter.
我们要认真对待这项工作（wǒ men yào rèn zhēn duì dài zhè xiàng gōng zuò）。
We should take this work seriously.
他会来的（tā huì lái de）。
He will come.

Here are some points that merit special attention.

1. Chinese verbs have no morphological changes whatsoever resulting from person, gender, number, time, etc.
我是医生（wǒ shì yī shēng）。
I'm a doctor.
她是护士（tā shì hù shì）。

She's a nurse.
他们是工人（tā men shì gōng rén）。
They are workers.
他正在写作业（tā zhèng zài xiě zuò yè）。
He is doing his homework.
他每天晚上写作业（tā měi tiān wǎn shàng xiě zuò yè）。
He does his homework every night.
他早就写了作业（tā zǎo jiù xiě le zuò yè）。
He did his homework earlier.

2. The particle 了（le）is suffixed to a verb to emphasize a competed action. For example:
我写了一本书（wǒ xiě le yì běn shū）。
I finished writing a book.
她走了（tā zǒu le）。
She left.

3. The particle 着（zhe）is suffixed to a verb to show a progressive action or continuous state. For example:
我开着车呢（wǒ kāi zhe chē ne）！
I'm currently driving (a vehicle).
窗户开着呢（chuāng hù kāi zhe ne）。
The window is opening.

4. The particle 过（guò）is suffixed to a verb to stress on a certain experience in the past. For example:
我看过这本书（wǒ kàn guò zhè běn shū）。
I have read this book before.
他之前干过翻译（tā zhī qián gàn guò fān yì）。
He used to be a translator.

Auxiliary Verb

The Chinese language doesn't have modal verb, but verbs that "help" other verbs to express necessity, possibility, and willingness. These verbs are called auxiliary verbs. Auxiliary verbs are often used to modify verbs or adjectives, and they are negated by 不(bù).

In addition, a noun cannot immediately follow them. The affirmative-negative question is formed by putting together the affirmative and negative forms of an auxiliary verb, and that question formed can be answered by the auxiliary verb directly. For example:

你能不能来（nǐ néng bù néng lái）？
Can you come or not?
能（néng）。
Yes, I can.
不能（bù néng）。
No, I cannot.
他想不想打游戏（tā xiǎng bù xiǎng dǎ yóu xì）？
Does he want to play video games or not?
想（xiǎng）。
Yes, he does.
不想（bù xiǎng）。
No, he doesn't.

Auxiliary verbs are often used as adverbial adjuncts before verbs and adjectives. Below we will introduce usage of some common anxiliary verbs.

1. Those expressing capability, for example:
能（néng）can, be capable of
我能办好这件事（wǒ néng bàn hǎo zhè jiàn shì）。
I can do this thing.
能够（néng gòu）can, be capable of, be able to
她能够做到（tā néng gòu zuò dào）。
She can make it.
会（huì）can, be able to
你会说中文吗（nǐ huì shuō zhōng wén ma）？
Can you speak Chinese?

2. Those expressing possibility, for example:
能 (néng) = may

我能进来吗（wǒ néng jìn lái ma）?
May I come in?

会（huì）will

她会来吗（tā huì lái ma）?
Will she come?

可以（kě yǐ）can, be able to

你不可以在这里吸烟（nǐ bú kě yǐ zài zhè lǐ xī yān）。
You can't smoke here.

可能（kě néng）might happen, possible, probable

天可能要下雨（tiān kě néng yào xià yǔ）。
It might rain.

3. Those expressing necessity by reason, for example:

应该（yīng gāi）ought to, should

你应该走了（nǐ yīng gāi zǒu le）。
You should leave now.

应当（yīng dāng）should, be supposed to

你不应当出现在这里（nǐ bù yīng dāng chū xiàn zài zhè lǐ）。
You are not supposed to be here.

该（gāi）should

我该吃药了（wǒ gāi chī yào le）。
I should take some medicine.

要（yào）must

我要去上班了（wǒ yào qù shàng bān le）。
I must go to work.

4. Those expressing obligation, for example:

必须（bì xū）have to, must

每个人都必须遵纪守法（měi gè rén dōu bì xū zūn jì shǒu fǎ）。
Everyone must abide by the law.

得（děi）need to, have to

你今天得把钱还给我（nǐ jīn tiān děi bǎ qián huán gěi wǒ）。
You have to pay me back today.

5. Those expressing willingness, for example:

要（yào）want to

她要去国外旅游（tā yào qù guó wài lǚ yóu）。

She wants to travel abroad.

想（xiǎng）want to, wish to

我想睡觉（wǒ xiǎng shuì jiào）。

I want to sleep.

愿意（yuàn yì）wish to, be willing to

他非常愿意做这件事（tā fēi cháng yuàn yì zuò zhè jiàn shì）。

He is very willing to do this thing.

敢（gǎn）dare to

她敢去挑战领导的权威（tā gǎn qù tiāo zhàn lǐng dǎo de quán wēi）。

She dares to challenge the authority of her supervisor.

肯（kěn）be willing to, be ready to

这孩子不肯回家（zhè hái zi bù kěn huí jiā）。

The child is unwilling to go back home.

Chapter 4: Numerals and Measure Words

Numerals

Words representing numbers are called numerals, such as: 一（yī）one
二（èr）two
三（sān）three
四（sì）four
五（wǔ）five
六（liù）six
七（qī）seven
八（bā）eight
九（jiǔ）nine
十（shí）ten
百（bǎi）hundred
千（qiān）thousand
万（wàn）ten thousand
亿（yì）a hundred million
零（líng）zero

两（liǎng）two

The above basic numerals can be combined with words to represent various kinds of numbers. Larger numbers in Chinese are especially logical.

Numbers from 11-19: 十（shí）+ number. For example: 十四（shí sì）fourteen

Multiples of 10: number + 十（shí）. For example: 五十（wǔ shí）fifty

From 21-29: 二十（èr shí）+ number. For example: 二十三（èr shí sān）twenty-three, and so forth. The same applies to larger numbers, for example 七十六（qī shí liù）seventy-six.

Hundreds: 100 is 一百（yī bǎi）, 200 is 两百（liǎng bǎi）, 300 is 三百（sān bǎi）, and so forth.

Thousands: 1,000 is 一千（yī qiān), 2,000 is 两千（liǎng qiān), 3,000 is 三千（sān qiān), and so forth.

Chinese has two words for "two".

èr is used in counting and in words for larger numbers. For example: 二十二（èr shí èr）twenty-two.

liǎng is used when you are talking about two of something. For example: 两个苹果（liǎng gè píng guǒ）two apples.

The 2 in numbers from 20-29 is always èr. While the 2 in numbers like 200 and 2,000 can either.

Ordinal numbers can be formed by placing the prefix 第（dì）before numerals. For example:

第一（dì yī）first

第十（dì shí）tenth

In some circumstances, however, numerals can bu put directly before nouns to act as ordinal numbers. For example:

三楼（sān lóu）the third floor

二哥（èr gē）second brother

Multiple numbers are formed by adding the measure word 倍（bèi）after numerals. For example:

一倍（yí bèi）one time

二十倍（èr shí bèi）twenty times

一千倍（yì qiān bèi）a thousand times

Decimals are shown by the formula number + 点（diǎn）+ number. The numbers before 点（diǎn）are the whole number and the figures after 点（diǎn）are the decimal places. For example:

零点三（líng diǎn sān）zero point three

十点七五（shí diǎn qī wǔ）ten point seventy five

Chinese uses number + 分之（fēn zhī）+ number to indicate fractions. The denominator is placed before the numerator. For example:

三分之二（sān fēn zhī èr）two thirds

十分之九（shí fēn zhī jiǔ）nine tenths

Now, let's have a tongue twister.

四是四，十是十 (sì shì sì, shí shì shí)。

十四是十四，四十是四十 (shí sì shì shí sì, sì shí shì sì shí)。

谁说十四是四，就打谁十四 (shuí shuō shí sì shì sí sì, jiù dǎ shuí shí sì)。

谁说四十是十，就打谁四十 (shuí shuō sì shí shì shí, jiù dǎ shuí sì shí)。

Fun, isn't it? Well, we don't provide translation here because this is only a tongue twister to entertain! If you want to figure out what this short tongue twister means, just keep studying this book with us!

Measure words

In Chinese, there is a special part of speech known as the measure word. It indicates the measure or unit of things or persons. In modern Chinese, a numeral may not qualify a noun by itself; there must be a measure word between the numeral and the noun. Almost everything can be "measured", represented by a specific measure word.

Therefore, it is imperative for foreign learners of Chinese to learn every noun with its matching measure word.

There are over two hundred measure words in Chinese. Normally people choose the measure word according to the appearance of the object. Some of the most important measure words are:

个（gè）

Used before a noun which does not have a fixed measure word of its own. It is the most common and multi-purpose nominal measure word. For example:

一个人（yí gè rén）one person

两个桔子（liǎng gè jú zi）two oranges

三个苹果（sān gè píng guǒ）three apples

种（zhǒng）kind, sort, type

这里有三种果汁（zhè lǐ yǒu sān zhǒng guǒ zhī）。
There are three types of juice.

我想买这种杯子（wǒ xiǎng mǎi zhè zhǒng bēi zi）。
I want to buy this kind of cup.

我不做那种工作（wǒ bú zuò nà zhǒng gōng zuò）。
I don't do that kind of work.

些，一些（xiē, yì xiē）some

这些（zhè xiē）these

那些（nà xiē）those

我要去超市买些水果（wǒ yào qù chāo shì mǎi xiē shuǐ guǒ）。
I need to buy some fruit from the supermarket.

你能不能借我一些钱（nǐ néng bù néng jiè wǒ yì xiē qián）？
Could you please lend me some money?

我不喜欢那些人（wǒ bù xǐ huān nà xiē rén）。
I don't like those people.

瓶（píng）bottle

一瓶水（yì píng shuǐ）a bottle of water

两瓶可乐（liǎng píng kě lè）two bottles of coke.

杯（bēi）cup

一杯茶（yì bēi chá）a cup of tea

三杯咖啡（sān bēi kā fēi）three cups of coffee

条（tiáo）

Used to describe something long, narrow, or thin. For example:

一条围巾（yì tiáo wéi jīn）a scarf

一条路（yì tiáo lù）a path

块（kuài）piece, lump

两块面包（liǎng kuài miàn bāo）two pieces of bread

几块冰（jǐ kuài bīng）a few pieces of ice

袋，包（dài，bāo）bag

两袋盐（liǎng dài yán）two bags of salt

四包饼干（sì bāo bǐng gān）four bags of cookies

本（běn）

Used to describe books, magazines, notebooks, etc. For example:

一本字典（yì běn zì diǎn）a dictionary

两本杂志（liǎng běn zá zhì）too magazines

张（zhāng）

Used to describe something with a flat surface. For example:

一张桌子（yì zhāng zhuō zi）a table

一张床（yì zhāng chuáng）a bed

Next, we will introduce you to the proper way to count Chinese money and express time.

The Chinese currency is Renminbi (RMB or CNY) and has two units: 元（yuán）or 块（kuài）and 角（jiǎo）or 毛（máo）.

元（yuán）is always used after an amount of money written in Arabic numerals. For example:

0.5元，0.5元钱，5角钱（líng diǎn wǔ yuán, líng diǎn wǔ yuán qián, wǔ jiǎo qián）50 cents

6.8元，6.8元钱，6元8角钱（liù diǎn bā yuán, liù diǎn bā yuán qián, liù yuán bā jiǎo qián）6 yuan and 80 cents

In spoken Chinese, the 钱（qián）in the above examples is often omitted. Moreover, 块（kuài） and 毛（máo）are more used in spoken Chinese and the last measure word can be omitted. For example:

五毛（wǔ máo）fifty cents

六块八（liù kuài bā）six *yuan* and eighty cents

To express time, Chinese has 年（nián），月（yuè），周（zhōu），星期（xīng qī），礼拜（lǐ bài），and 日（rì）or 号（hào）.

To indicate years, the pattern is: number + 年（nián）

For example:

今年是二零二零年（jīn nián shì èr líng èr líng nián）。
This year is 2020.

这个国家有两千年历史（zhè gè guó jiā yǒu liǎng qiān nián lì shǐ）。
This country has a history of 2,000 years.

For months of the year, the pattern is: number + 月（yuè）

一月（yī yuè）January

二月（èr yuè）February

三月（sān yuè）March

四月（sì yuè）April

五月（wǔ yuè）May

六月（liù yuè）June

七月（qī yuè）July

八月（bā yuè）August

九月（jiǔ yuè）September

十月（shí yuè）October

十一月（shí yī yuè）November

十二月（shí èr yuè）December

Names for days of the week are formed using the pattern 星期（xīng qī）+ number, 礼拜（lǐ bài）+ number, or 周（zhōu）+ number. Sunday is an exception.

星期一（xīng qī yī） Monday
星期二（xīng qī èr） Tuesday
星期三（xīng qī sān） Wednesday
星期四（xīng qī sì） Thursday
星期五（xīng qī wǔ） Friday
星期六（xīng qī liù） Saturday
星期天（xīng qī tiān） Sunday

For all of the above, 周（zhōu） or 礼拜（lǐ bài） can be substituted for 星期（xīng qī）.

To express date, the pattern is number + 日（rì） or 号（hào）. 号（hào） is more common in colloquial language. For example:

今天是一月十一号（jīn tiān shì yī yuè shí yī hào）。
Today is January 11th.

今天是二月十二日（jīn tiān shì èr yuè shí èr rì）。
Today is Feburary 12th.

In Chinese, a date is given in the following order: Year-Month-Date. Therefore, if you want to express your birthday, you should say:

我的生日是1995年2月28日（wǒ de shēng rì shì yī jiǔ jiǔ wǔ nián èr yuè èr shí bā rì）。
I was born on Feb 28th, 1995.

Chapter 5: Auxiliary Words

Chinese words can be divided into two categories according to their meaning and grammatical function – notional words and auxiliary words. Notional words have actual meaning and can act as independent sentence elements. We already learned about notional words in Chapter 2 to 4. Auxiliary words do not have actual meaning and can not be used alone as sentence elements. Adverbs, prepositions, conjunctions, particles, interjections, and onamatopes are in this category. The use of auxiliary words plays an important role in the Chinese language. Though these words do not carry concrete lexical meaning, they are grammatically important. Let's discuss them one by one.

Adverbs
A word generally used in front of a verb or adjective to express time, degree, scope, repetition, negation, possibility, or tone of speech, etc. is called an adverb. Adverbs cannot be used as modifier of a noun or be reduplicated. Moreover, most of them cannot be used alone to answer a question or precede subjects.

The basic use of an adverb is to serve as adverbial adjunct. As an adverbial adjunct, the adverb is always placed before a verb or an adjective and never after. For example:

他今天特别高兴（tā jīn tiān tè bié gāo xìng）。
He's really happy today.
这个女孩真漂亮（zhè gè nǚ hái zhēn piào liàng）。
This girl is very ptetty.

Prepositons

A word that can be put before a noun or pronoun to form a prepositional phrase indicating time, place, direction, object, reason, manner, passive, comparison, or exclusion, etc. is called a preposition. Generally speaking, a preposition cannot be an element of a sentence by itself. Most prepositions must take a noun or a pronoun to form a prepositional phrase to serve as an adverbial adjunct, complement or attributive, for example:

As an adverbial adjunct:
他从北方来（tā cóng běi fāng lái）。
He's from the north.

As an attributive:
这是关于月亮的传说（zhè shì guān yú yuè liàng de chuán shuō）。
This legend is about moon.

As a complement:
这列火车开往深圳（zhè liè huǒ chē kāi wǎng shēn zhèn）。
This train is heading toward Shenzhen.

Conjunctions

A conjunction is a word that can be joined with two words, phrases, or sentences to indicate the grammatical relation of coordination, causality, condition, supposition, etc. For example:

Coordination:
和，跟，同，与，及，并（hé, gēn, tóng, yǔ, jí, bìng）and

Causality:
因为（yīn wèi）because
所以（suǒ yǐ）so
因此（yīn cǐ）therefore

Condition:
只要（zhī yào）as long as

只有（zhī yǒu）only

不管（bù guǎn）despite

Supposition

如果，要是，假如，假设（rú guǒ, yào shì, jiǎ rú, jiǎ shè）if

Inference:

既然（jì rán）since, now that

这样（zhè yàng）like this

那么（nà me）in that way

Transition:

虽然（suī rán）though

但是（dàn shì）but

可是，不过（kě shì, bú guò）however

Concession:

即使（jí shǐ）even if

Alternative:

还是，或者（hái shì, huò zhě）or

Enumeration:

例如（lì rú）for example

比如（bǐ rú）such as

Succession:

接着，然后（jiē zhe, rán hòu）then

Progression:

甚至（shèn zhì）even

Particles

A word which is added to another word, phrase, or sentence to indicate various supplementary meanings, grammatical relations, or mood is called a particle. Particles can be divided into three kinds.

1. Structural particles

Particles added to words or phrases to indicate grammatical relations are called structural particles. The most important structural particles are:

的（de）as in 我的书（wǒ de shū）my book.

地（de）as in 高兴地说（gāo xìng de shuō）happily say
得（de）as in 跑得快（pǎo de kuài）run fast

2. Aspectual particles

Particles added to verbs to indicate a supplementary meaning are called aspectual particles. The aspectual particles are:

了（le）
Suffixed to a verb indicating the completion of an action.
他走了（tā zǒu le）。
He left.

着（zhe）
Indicates that an action is in progress or in a certain state at a certain time, or a certain state is continuing.
她在房间唱着歌（tā zài fáng jiān chàng zhe gē）。
She's singing in the room.

过（guo）
Indicates that an action took place in the past.
我去过美国（wǒ qù guo měi guó）。
I have been to America.

3. Modal particles

Particles used at the end of a sentence to express moods are:
吗（ma）呢（ne）吧（ba）啊（a）嘛（ma）啦（la）呀（ya）哇（wa）

When not knowing something and expecting an answer, the speaker can put 吗（ma）at the end of a statement. For example:
你好吗（nǐ hǎo ma）？
How are you?
抽屉里有笔吗（chōu tì lǐ yǒu bǐ ma）？
Is there any pen in the drawer?

呢（ne）can be used at the end of an affirmative-negative sentence to indicate a tone of uncertainty. For example:
她能不能来呢（tā néng bù néng lái ne）？
Will she be able to come?

呢（ne）can be used at the end of a question with an interrogative pronoun to indicate a tone of conjecture. For example:
这是谁的书呢（zhè shì shuí de shū ne）?
Whose book is this?
呢（ne）can be used at the end of an alternative question to suggest a tone of releasing or urging.
你喜欢英语还是喜欢法语呢（nǐ shì xué yīng yǔ hái shì xué fǎ yǔ ne）?
Do you like English or French?

Interjections

An interjection is a word which can express an exclamation, a call or a reponse. It doesn't have a concrete meaning. It only indicates a kind of feeling or a sound that draws attention. Interjections are quite independent and have no grammatical relationships with other parts of the sentence. They usually occur at the beginning of a sentence. For example:
喂（wèi）嗯（èn）啊（á，à）哎（āi）噢（ō）哦（ò）唉（ài）
Each interjection expresses a certain feeling or imitates a certain sound, so it cannot be used indiscriminately. Here are some interjection use cases:
喂（wèi）is used when answering a phone call.
嗯（èn）indicates response.
啊（á）indicates surprise.
啊（à）indicates admiration.
哎（āi）is used when friends say hello to each other.
噢（ō）or 哦（ò）indicates realization and awakening.
唉（ài）is the sound of a sigh.

Onomatopes

An onomatope is a word which imitates the sound of a thing or an action. It doesn't have concrete meaning but only indicates a sound. For example:
哗哗（huá huá）thesound of water flowing

哈哈（hā hā）the sound of laughter
呼呼（hū hū）the sound of wind
汪汪（wāng wāng）dogs barking
扑通（pū tōng）sound of a big weight falling onto the ground or into the water

PART TWO: GRAMMAR

Chapter 6: Phrases and Sentence Elements

Phrases

A sentence is composed of words and phrases. Phrases are combinations of grammatically related words, and like words, function as sentence elements. Some phrases can also stand alone as a sentence. Phrases are sometimes called construtions. There are a variety of phrases in Chinese, of which the following 11 are commonly used:

1. The coordinative phrase

A coordinative phrase is one formed by two or more words of the same part of speech in coordinative relation. The order of the two constituents is not fixed. Reversion of the order does not affect the meaning. A coordinative phrase is usually composed of nouns, pronouns, verbs, or adjectives. For example:

老师学生（lǎo shī xué shēng）teachers and students

他和我（tā hé wǒ）he and I

又唱又跳（yòu chàng yòu tiào）sing and dance

高大帅气（gāo dà shuài qì）tall and handsome

2. The subject-predicate phrase

A subject-predicate phrase is one in which the constituents are combined in the relation. The order of the two constituents is fixed with the subject preceding the predicate. The first constituent of the phrase is usually a noun or pronoun serving as a topic or the subject, and the second one, usually a verb or an adjective, is the predicate describing the subject. The resersion of order will bring about a change both in structure and in meaning. For example:

头发长（tóu fa cháng）hair is long

长头发（cháng tóu fa）long hair

目的明确（mù de míng què）the destination is clear

明确目的（míng què mù de）to know the destination

3. The verb-object phrase

A verb-pbject phrase is one in which the constituents are combined in the relation. The order of constituents of the phase is fixed, and the verb precedes the object. For example:

吃早饭（chī zǎo fàn）eat breakfast

写汉字（xiě hàn zi）write Chinese character

4. The endocentric phrase

An endocentric phrase is one in which the constituents are combined so that the first modifies the second, and the order of the two constituents can not be reversed. The reversion of order will lead to a change both in structure and in meaning, or even make the phrase logically or grammatically unsound. For example:

很结实（hěn jié shi）very strong

太晚（tài wǎn）too late

他哥哥（tā gē ge）his older brother

5. The numeral-measure phrase

A phrase which is the combination of a numeral and a measure word is called a numeral-measure word phrase. The order of the two constituents in the phrase is fixed: the numeral always precedes the measure word, and this order cannot be reversed. For example:

三本书（sān běn shū）three books

两支笔（liǎng zhī bǐ）two pens

However, one can say 书三本（shū sān běn）or 笔两支（bǐ liǎng zhī）in statistics.

6. The complementary phrase

A complementary phrase is one in which the constituents are combined in a complementary relationship. It can be formed by a verb and its complement or an adjective and its complement. The complement may be a verb, adjective, and in a few cases, an adverb or a phrase. The order of the two constituents in the phrase is fixed. For example:

感觉真棒（gǎn jué zhēn bàng）feel great

危险得很（wēi xiǎn de hěn）incredibly dangerous

7. The locality phrase

The phrase of locality is one where the noun of locality is a modified word indicating place, position, time, or quantity. The order of the two constituents can not be reversed, for the reversion will lead to a change of meaning. For example:

三天前（sān tiān qián）three days before

前三天（qián sān tiān）the first three days

屋里（wū lǐ）in the room

里屋（lǐ wū）the inner room

8. The appositive phrase

A combination of two words which refer to the same person or thing from different aspects, and where each adds some information to the other is called an appositive phrase. The order of the two constituents is fixed, with the emphasis on the second one. For example:

你们三个（nǐ men sān gè）you three

我朋友保罗（wǒ péng yǒu bǎo luó）my friend Paul

9. The set phrase

A set phrase, such as a proper noun, a technical term, an idiom, etc. is one which is composed of fixed constituents to express a specific concept and is used as a while. None of the constituents in a set phrase can be substituted and they are arranged in a fixed order. For example:

有其父必有其子（yǒu qí fù bì yǒu qí zǐ）like father like son

爱屋及乌（ài wū jí wū）love me love my dog

中华人民共和国（zhōng huá rén mín gòng hé guó）The People's Republic of China

了如指掌（liǎo rú zhǐ zhǎng）to know something like the palm of one's hand

开诚布公（kāi chéng bù gōng）to speak frankly and sincerely

10. The prepositional phrase

The prepositional phrase is formed by a preposition and its object. It refers to directions, place, position, time, object, purpose, reason, or maner of an action, and expresses passivity, comparison, disposal, or exclusion etc. The word order of a prepositional phrase is fixed: the preposition always precedes its object. Nouns, pronouns, numeral-measure phrase, nouns, phrases of locality, time nouns, or nominal endocentric phrases can serve as a prepositonal object. For example:

除了这座城市（chú le zhè zuò chéng shì）except this city

在网上（zài wǎng shàng）on the internet

从美国（cóng měi guó）from America

11. The 的（de）phrase

The 的（de）phrase is one in which the structural particle 的（de）is attached to a notional word or phrase which refers to a person or thing. In the phrase, as a rule, 的（de）must be suffixed to the other constituent. The phrase functions as a noun in a sentence. For example:

这是他给我的（zhè shì tā gěi wǒ de）。

He gave me this.

他给我的是一本书（tā gěi wǒ de shì yì běn shū）。

What he gave me is a book.

她是来参加表演的（tā shì lái cān jiā biǎo yǎn de）。

She is coming for the show.
参加表演的在里面（cān jiā biǎo yǎn de zài lǐ miàn）。
Those coming to the show are inside.

All in all, we distinguish the various phrases according to the following features:

1. In terms of parts of speech, grammatical relations, and meanings of their constituents.
2. In terms of whether their constituents are arranged in a fixed order.
3. In terms of the ways in which their constituents are connected, ie. Whether conjunctions are employed and if so, what kind of conjunctions are employed.
4. In terms of whether the phrase can be preceded or followed by other elements and what these elements are.

Sentence Elements

A sentence is the smallest language unit of communication that can be used by itself to express an idea. Sentences are composed of words and phrases arranged according to certain grammatical relationships which can include several sentence elements in line with their syntax functions. Generally, there are six sentence elements: subject, predicate, object, attributive, adverbial adjunct, and complement. Words or phrases can act as sentence elements. Do you remember how many kinds of Chinese words and phrases we've learned above?

1. Subject

In Chinese, the subject of a sentence is determined by its position and meaning. Usually the subject, which is the theme of a statement, occurs at the beginning of a sentence before the predicate. There is not any particular marker for the subject in Chinese. Words or phrases can serve as subjects with out any change in form, even verbs or verbal phrases functioning as subject are not market by any words such as pronouns etc., and the form of the verbs will remain unchanged. For example:

学习中文很有意思（xué xí zhōng wén hěn yǒu yì si）。

Learning Chinese is very interesting.

受人帮助道谢是一种礼节（shòu rén bāng zhù dào xiè shì yì zhǒng lǐ jié）。

It is polite to say thanks to those that help you.

Another important feature is that subjects in most sentences are doers of actions, the ones that launch the action. But there are some other cases, instead of launching the action, the subjects receive the actions, they are the receivers of actions. Such cases are common in Chinese, and they do not have to be a passive sentence.

房间打扫干净了（fáng jiān dǎ sǎo gàn jìng le）。

The room has been cleaned.

作业写完了（zuò yè xiě wán le）。

The homework has been finished.

2. Predicate

Relationships between a subject and predicate are various. The predicate indicates an action done or received by the subject, describes, explains, or makes a judgement of the subject, expressing what the subject is, what it does, or how it is. For example:

她是我妻子（tā shì wǒ qī zi）。

She's my wife.

树叶黄了（shù yè huáng le）。

The leaves are turning yellow.

玛丽又迟到了（mǎ lì yòu chí dào le）。

Mary is late again.

3. Object

There are various relationships between the object and verb predicates. In terms of meaning and function, the object can be the doer or receiver of an action, the result or influence of an action, the destination of an action, or the instrument with which an action is done.

Words or phrases are used as objects without any morphological marker. With verbs, verb-object phrases, coordinative or endocentric verbal phrases, or subject-predicate phrases function as the object, no preposition or pronoun is required and the verb in these phrases remains unchanged in form this is very important. For example:

我们需要休息（wǒ men xū yào xiū xi）。
We need to take a rest.

我需要休息一会儿（wǒ xū yào xiū xi yì huìr）。
I need to rest for a while.

Some verbs take two objects, which are called double objects. The first one, mostly a personal noun or pronoun, is called an indirect object and the second one, mostly a noun or phrase of non-personal reference, is called a direct object. For example:

我送她一件礼物（wǒ sòng tā yí jiàn lǐ wù）。
I gave her a present.

她教我们英语（tā jiāo wǒ men yīng yǔ）。
She teaches us English.

You may notice that in the above examples no auxiliary word is used between the two objects, but their order is fixed: the indirect object (referring to person) is followed by the direct object (of non-personal reference).

In Chinese, most objects are receivers of actions, but some objects are the active doers of actions. Objects that do actions often appear in such sentences: beginning words or phrases denoting place or time are used to indicate the existence, appearance, or disappearance of a thing or a person. If the objects are people, living animals, or plants, they are objects that do actions. For example:

昨天我家来了两位客人（zuó tiān wǒ jiā lái le liǎng wèi kè rén）。
Yesterday my home came two guests. (I had two guests visiting me yesterday.)

门口站着一个人（mén kǒu zhàn zhe yí gè rén）。
By the door is standing a person. (There is a person standing by the door.)

4. Attributive

A word or phrase which modifies or restricts the subject or object is called an attributive and the word modified by the attributibe is called the head word. In other words, the attributive is the premodifier showing the property, quality, quantity, category, place, time, or scope of what is denoted by the head word. It must be noted that the attributive must be placed before the head word it modifies and this order cannot be reversed, as the reversion of order will lead to a change of structure and meaning, or will even make the phrase senseless. For example:

左边的房子（zuǒ biān de fáng zi）the house on the left

房子的左边（fáng zi de zuǒ biān）on the left of the house

厚外套（hòu wài tào）thick coat

外套厚（wài tào hòu）the coat is thick

今天的报纸（jīn tiān de bào zhǐ）today's newspaper

5. Adverbial adjunct

A word or phrase modifying or restricting a predicate is called an adverbial adjunct and the word it modifies is the head word. In other words, the adverbial adjunct is the premodifying element denoting the time, place, degree, scope, aspect, affirmation or negation, repetition, activeness or passiveness, target, reason, etc. of the head word. What should be noted is that adverbial adjuncts must precede, not follow, the head words which they modify or restrict. For example:

他不喜欢打篮球（tā bù xǐ huān dǎ lán qiú）。

He doesn't like to play basketball.

我们用汉语交流（wǒ men yòng hàn yǔ jiāo liú）。

We communicate with each other in Chinese.

Two or more adverbs are often used in succession as adverbial adjuncts. When thus used, attention should be paid to their order: the modifier always precedes the modified and this order can not be reversed. Otherwise, the meaning will be changed, become illogical, or ungrammatical. For example:

十年前的这件事我已经不记得了（shí nián qián de zhè jiàn shì wǒ yǐ jīng bú jì dé le）。

I don't remember the thing happened ten years ago.

很多大学生都经常兼职（hěn duō dà xué shēng dōu jīng cháng jiān zhí）。
Many college students often take part time jobs.

6. Complement

A word or phrase attached to a verb or adjective predicate to complete the meaning is called a complement. Complements are postmodifying elements to show the duration, quantity, degree, result, direction or possibility of an action; or to illustrate the state, number, degree of a thing.

The grammatical feathres of complements are: the complement always comes after the head word; mainly adjectives, vers, numeral-measure word phrases, complementary phrases, etc. can act as complements; the structural particle 得（de）often occurs between the head word and the complement; uaually a verb predicate with a complement can take an object.

In terms of both meaning and structure, complements can be classified into five types: result, degree, quantity, direction, and potentiality.

Chapter 7: Simple and Complex Sentences

A sentence is composed of words or phrases arranged according to certain grammatical rules to express a comparatively complete meaning along with certain tones and intonations. In connected discourse, there is a stop between each two sentences which is indicated by a full stop in writing. Sentences can be divided into two categories: simple and complex.

Simple Sentences

A simple sentence usually consists of two sections: the subject section and the predicate section, with the former preceding the latter. It may contain one word, several words, or phrases.

Senctences can be classified, in terms of whether they contain one or two sections, into the subject-predicate sentences and the non-subject-predicate sentences.

A sentence containing the subject section and the predicate section is called a subject-predicate sentence. For example:

这里真安静（zhè lǐ zhēn ān jìng）。
It's really quiet here.
他们是交换生（tā men shì jiāo huàn shēng）。

They're an exchange student.

A sentence is called a non-subject-predicate if it does not contain or cannot be divided into the subject and the predicate sections. For example:

人呢（rén ne）？

Anyone here?

看（kàn）！

Look!

禁止吸烟（jìn zhǐ xī yān）。

No smoking.

The simple sentence expresses different meanings and tones such as a declaration, interrogation, etc. Sentences can be classified in terms of function and tone into four types: declarative, interrogative, imperative and exclamatory.

The declarative sentence is one used to state a thing or view. The sentence is uttered in the declarative tone and a full stop is written at the end. The declarative sentence may be one in the subject-predicate structure or in the non-subject-predicate structure. For example:

这是我的车（zhè shì wǒ de chē）。

This is my car.

今天天气真好（jīn tiān tiān qì zhēn hǎo）。

Today is a fine day.

开始（kāi shǐ）！

Begin!

An interrogative sentence is one used to ask a question, or a sentence uttered in the interrogative tone with a question mark written at the end. There are five major types of interrogative sentences:

1. Yes or no question: expecting yes or no as its answer. For example:

这是你的吗（zhè shì nǐ de ma）？

Is this yours?

2. Questions using interrogative pronouns: ask about a specific person, object, or other thing. For example:

他去哪里了（tā qù nǎ lǐ le）？
Where is he?

3. Affirmative and negative questions: formed by putting the affirmative and negative forms of the predicate together. Answers expected are either affirmative or negative. For example:
你要不要买这个（nǐ yào bú yào mǎi zhè ge）？
Will you buy this or not?

4. Alternative questions: questions in which several alternatives are paralleled by the conjunction 还是（hái shì） for the answerer to choose. For example:
你喜欢这红色的外套还是黑色得（nǐ xǐ huān zhè hóng sè de wài tào hái shì hēi sè de）？
Which coat do you like? The red one or the black one?

5. Rhetorical questions: questions to retort or to exaggerate. For example:
他不是个老师吗（tā bú shì ge lǎo shī ma）？
He is a teacher, isn't he?

The imperative sentence is one that expresses a command, request, urging, advice, warning, or consultation and has an imperative tone. At the end of such a sentence, a full stop or an exclamation mark is used. The subject is often absent in an imperative sentence. For example:
请进（qǐng jìn）。
Please come in.
快点（kuài diǎn）！
Hurry up!

The exclamatory sentence is a sentence that expresses praise, fondness, surprise, detestation, etc. and has an exclamatory tone. The exclamation mark is used at the end. Adverbs expressing high degrees such as 多么（duō me），真（zhēn），太（tài），etc. are often used in an exclamatory sentence as adverbial adjuncts or complements. For example:
这城市真大（zhè chéng shì zhēn dà）！

What a big city this is!
我太累了（wǒ tài lèi le）！
I'm so tired!

Complex sentences

Sentences consisting of two or more simple sentences, expressing a complete meaning and spoken in a certain intonation are called complex sentences. Simple sentences contained in a complex sentence are called clasues. Complex sentences can also be very simple, and simple sentences can be complex too. For example:
你刚走，她就来了（nǐ gāng zǒu, tā jiù lái le）。
She came just when you left.
风停了，雨也不下了（fēng tíng le, yǔ yě bú xià le）。
When the wind stopped, the rain stopped.

A complex sentence contains two or more clauses between which there is a pause. The pause is indicated by a comma or sometimes by a semicolon in writing. When the whole sentence is spoken, there should be a stop which is indicated in writing by a full stop, a question mark, or an exclamation mark. The sentence is spoken intonationally as a complete whole.

The clauses in a complex sentence may be various kinds of subject-predicate sentences. If the clauses share the same subject, then the subject does not have to be repeated. Some complex sentences may not have subject. For example:
她会英语，她还会法语（tā huì yīng yǔ, tā hái huì fǎ yǔ）。
She can speak English, and also speak French.
这本小说没意思，我不想看了（zhè běn xiǎo shuō méi yì si, wǒ bù xiǎng kàn le）。
This novel is boring. I don't want to read it.
他今天很忙，不能陪你出去（tā jīn tiān hěn máng, bù néng péi nǐ chū qù）。
He is too busy to go out with you today.

In a complex sentence, clauses have various relationships which are often denoted by correlatives. For example:

因为今天是周末,所以公园里人特别多(yīn wéi jīn tiān shì zhōu mò, suǒ yǐ gōng yuán lǐ rén tè bié duō)。
Because today is the weekend, there are a lot of people at the park.

我们不仅要好好学习,还要锻炼好身体(wǒ men bù jǐn yào hǎo hǎo xué xí, hái yào duàn liàn hǎo shēn tǐ)。
We must not only study hard, but also exercise well.

PART THREE: CONVERSATION

Conversation is the heart of language learning. Talking with someone in another language develops your listening skills while giving you the speaking practice that you need. Conversing in another language can be hard to manage when are first starting out. In this section, not only will we guide, but also your language partner as well. Conversation is all about improvising within the linguistc and cultural rules of the language. This part allows you to improvise with a manageable number of high frequency questions and answers and gives your language partner a guide as to how to help you so that you can both make the most of your time. Below are some suggestions on how to use this section.
1. Read it all the way through. It gives you a unique perspective on the grammar at work behind the patterns and characters used in the questions and answers.
2. Personalize it. Take some time to personalize the questions and answers in this part with your own personal details. If someone asks you one of these questions, it is important for you to be able to come up with a suitable personal response. Write out your answers or your likely answers to each of the questions and keep that list handy.
3. Chat. Whether you are face to face or texting, communicating with real people is still the best way to learn a language. You need to use the questions and answers in this part as often as you can. You

don't need to be perfect. In fact, you'll have to make mistakes in order to learn languages. No one, native speaker or foreigner, young or old, has ever learned Mandarin without going through the same things that you are going through right now. If you have a language partner, let the person know that you are focusing on these questions and answers and give the person a copy of them so he or she can help you. You will be able to make the most of your time if both of you are using these questions and answers in your conversations.

Chapter 8: Basic Greetings

Saying "hello" is the first step to start a conversation. We believe that the first word you are taught in class or textbook regarding greetings is你好(nǐ hǎo). Are you saying你好(nǐ hǎo) to greet just about anyone you encounter? There is actually a variety of different ways to say "hello" in Chinese. 你好(nǐ hǎo) is often used to greet strangers, and is not used by native Chinese on daily basis. Now, let's learn some typical ones.

吃了吗（chī le ma）?

Have you eaten?

你胖了（nǐ pàng le）！

You're getting fat.

You may find the first sentence strange. Why are people asking me about my meals? Will they invite me for a meal? In actuality, this is just a way to show that the speaker cares about you. Having meals on time is really important in traditional Chinese culture; therefore, many people often start the conversation with this sentence.

You may find the third sentence rude. The literal translation is rude indeed. How can you just say that to my face? But actually, the speaker means that you are eating well, sleeping well, working well… that everything is going well around you, that you look fabulous.

You can use these two greetings with your friends, relatives, or other people you already know well. If you still use你好(nǐ hǎo) to greet these people, it may be too distant and polite.

Formal greetings in Chinese are really the same as greetings in English. The difference may only the word order. For example:

早（zǎo）!
Morning!

早上好（zǎo shàng hǎo）!
Good morning!

下午好（xià wǔ hǎo）!
Good afternoon!

晚上好（wǎn shàng hǎo）!
Good evening!

晚安（wǎn ān）!
Good night!

好久不见（hǎo jiǔ bú jiàn）!
Long time no see!

你好吗（nǐ hǎo ma）?
How are you?

很高兴认识你（hěn gāo xìng rèn shí nǐ）。
Nice to meet you.

很高兴见到你（hěn gāo xìng jiàn dào nǐ）。
Glad to see you.

代我向你父母问好（dài wǒ xiàng nǐ fù mǔ wèn hǎo）。
Please send my regards to your parents.

再见（zài jiàn）!
Goodbye!

一路顺风（yí lù shùn fēng）!
Have a nice trip!

Chinese people like to use informal greetings in cases where they don't need to use formal greetings. Therefore, as a language learner, we're supposed to greet someone in a Chinese way when speaking Chinese. Here are some more informal Chinese informal:

嘿（hèi）!
Hey!

哈喽（hā lou）!
Hello!

干啥去（gàn shá qù）?
Where are you going?

忙啥呢（máng shá ne）?
What are you busy with?

最近咋样（zuì jìn zǎ yàng）? / 近来如何（jìn lái rú hé）?
How's everything going lately?

家里还好吧（jiā lǐ hái hǎo ba）?
Is your family well?

出去呀（chū qù ya）?
Going out?

回来了（huí lái le）?
You're back?

Through English translations, you may feel these are nothing special. But we assure you, if you use these sentences to greet your Chinese friends or colleagues (don't use these sentences to greet your supervisors or boss) instead of 你好（nǐ hǎo）, they will be quite happy.

Now you're ready to greet people. Happy chatting.

Chapter 9: Introducing Yourself

We strongly recommend you choose a Chinese name, just as many Chinese people choose an English name. This action will directly shorten the distance between you and your listener.

Chinese naming conventions are quite different from what we know in the west. First names are created rather than picked from a list or passed down. A typical first name is made up of two characters, which is pronounced as two syllables, and they tend to carry some meaning. This is similar to native American naming conventions. There are thousands of characters to choose from, so first names tend to be unique. However, due to China's great population, many people have same names (not only same first name, but also last name).

There is no real list of most common Chinese first names, but last names are a different story. The Chinese present themselves with their last names first. There really aren't all that many different last names in China – about 100 or so are common. Here is a list of the top 10:

李（lǐ）

王（wáng）

张（zhāng）

刘（liú）

陈（chén）

杨（yáng）

赵（zhào）

黄（huáng）

周（zhōu）

吴（wú）

There are several ways to ask someone's name in Chinese, but we'll be taking a look at the most common ones. Let's check out the question first.

你叫什么名字（nǐ jiào shén me míng zi）?

What is your name?

您贵姓（nín guì xìng）?

May I have your family name please?

From the English translations, we can see that the first question is quite casual while the second is quite formal. Therefore, you will hear people ask the first question in everyday life, and the second in very formal occasions. So, what are the answers? Let's use a typical Chinese name – 李小龙（lǐ xiǎo lóng）in our examples.

The answer to the first question:

我叫李小龙（wǒ jiào lǐ xiǎo lóng）。

I'm Li Xiaolong./My name is Li Xiaolong.

The answer to the second question:

免贵姓李（miǎn guì xìng lǐ）。

Please just call me Li.

After knowing your name, another question follows, and that is to ask where you are from:

你是哪国人（nǐ shì nǎ guó rén）? or 你从哪里来（nǐ cóng nǎ lǐ lái）?

Here we are literally asking "you are which country person?" or "You from where come?" Although the literal translation sounds awkard in English, it is easy to see how the words match up.

Then, how do you say your nationality?

Pattern: 我是（wǒ shì）+ country name + 人（rén）
For example:
我是美国人（wǒ shì měi guó rén）。
I'm American.
我是德国人（wǒ shì dé guó rén）。
I'm German.
我是意大利人（wǒ shì yì dà lì rén）。
I'm Italian.
我是日本人（wǒ shì rì běn rén）。
I'm Japanese.
And how do you say, "I am from…"?
Pattern: someone + 是（shì）+ 从（cóng）+ country/city/place + 来的（lái de）
For example:
我是从英国来的（wǒ shì cóng yīng guó lái de）。
I'm from England.
她是从北京来的（tā shì cóng běi jīng lái de）。
She's from Beijing.
我朋友是从澳大利亚来的（wǒ péng yǒu shì cóng ào dà lì yà lái de）。
My friend comes from Australia.
Other than questions, here are more things you can introduce about yourself or your family.
How to tell someone "where you do something"?
Pattern: subject + 在（zài）+ place + predicate
For example:
我在北京大学教数学（wǒ zài běi jīng dà xué jiāo shù xué）。
I teach math in Peking University.
她在加拿大工作（tā zài jiā ná dà gōng zuò）。
She works in Canada.
In Chinese word order, the place must come before the predicate. In other words, while in English you can say "I work in China," in

Chinese you must say 我在中国工作（wǒ zài zhōng guó gōng zuò）; it is incorrect to say 我工作在中国（wǒ gōng zuò zài zhōng guó）.

How do you say what someone does for a living?

There are three patterns. The first one is who + 是（shì）+ name of profession. It is used to say someone "is a" teacher, student, doctor, etc. For example:

我姐姐是护士（wǒ jiě jie shì hù shì）。
My older sister is a nurse.

我老公是警察（wǒ lǎo gōng shì jǐng chá）。
My husband is a policeman.

The second one is who + 在（zài）+ place + 工作（gōng zuò）. It is used to say someone "works at/in" a school, hospital, library, etc. For example:

我爸爸在工厂工作（wǒ bà ba zài gōng chǎng gōng zuò）。
My father works in a factory.

你哥哥在阿里巴巴工作吗（nǐ gē ge zài ā lǐ bā bā gōng zuò ma）?
Does your older brother work at Alibaba?

The third one is who + 做（zuò）+ name of profession. It is used to say someone "works as a" doctor, driver, actor, etc. This pattern is often used in sentences where "to work as" follows another verb or adjective. For example:

你想做科学家吗（nǐ xiǎng zuò kē xué jiā ma）?
Do you want to be a scientist?

你想不想做演员（nǐ xiǎng bù xiǎng zuò yǎn yuán）?
Do you want to become an actor?

How to talk about your hobbies?

Pattern: 我的爱好是（wǒ de ài hào shì）… For example:

我的爱好是唱歌（wǒ de ài hào shì chàng gē）。
I like singing./My hobby is to sing.

我的爱好是钓鱼（wǒ de ài hào shì diào yú）。
I like fishing./My hobby is to go fishing.

To help you make a complete introduction, here are two paragraphs you can work on. After mastering the language, you can replace the details with yours.

Simple (you can use this in your daily life):

我叫李小龙。我是中国人。三年前，我在美国教中文。现在我在中国当翻译。我的父亲已经退休了，母亲在中学做老师。我喜欢打篮球和踢足球。

wǒ jiào lǐ xiǎo long. wǒ shì zhōng guó rén. sān nián qián, wǒ zài měi guó jiāo zhōng wén. xiàn zài wǒ zài zhōng guó dāng fān yì. wǒ de fù qīn yǐ jīng tuì xiū le, mǔ qīn zài zhōng xué zuò lǎo shī. wǒ xǐ huān dǎ lán qiú hé tī zú qiú.

I'm Li Xiaolong. I'm from China. Three years ago, I taught Chinese in America. Now, I work as a translator in China. My father has retired from work, and my mother works at a middle school. I like play basketball and football.

Hard (you can use this in a job interview):

下午好！我的名字是李小龙。今天有机会进行自我介绍深感荣幸。我乐意回答你们所提出来的任何问题。我希望我今天能表现的非常出色。我今年三十岁，出生在北京。我有很多兴趣爱好，如唱歌、跳舞、画画等。我目前是一家外贸公司的部门经理。我觉得自己是个工作勤奋、负责、能干，而且外向的人。依我的资格和经验，我觉得我对所从事的每一个项目都很努力、负责、勤勉。我的分析能力和与人相处的技巧，对贵单位必有价值。我希望能获得一份更好的工作，如果机会来临，我会抓住。我的工作经验使我适合这份工作。并且我相信我能成功。

xià wǔ hǎo! wǒ de míng zi shì lǐ xiǎo long. jīn tiān yǒu jī huì jìn xíng zì wǒ jiè shào shēn gǎn róng xìng. wǒ lè yì huí dá nǐ men suǒ tí chū lái de rèn hé wèn tí. wǒ xī wàng wǒ jīn tiān néng biǎo xiàn de fēi cháng chū sè. wǒ jīn nián sān shí suì, chū shēng zài běi jīng. wǒ yǒu hěn duō xìng qù ài hào, rú chàng gē, tiào wǔ, huà huà děng. wǒ mù qián shì yì jiā wài mào gōng sī de bù mén jīng lǐ. yī wǒ de zī gé hé jīng yàn, wǒ jué de wǒ duì suǒ cóng shì de měi yí gè xiàng mù dōu hěn nǔ lì, fù zé, qín miǎn. wǒ de fēn xī néng lì hé yǔ rén xiàng chǔ de jì qiǎo, duì guì dān wèi bì yǒu jià zhí. wǒ xī wàng néng huò dé yí fèn gèng hǎo de gōng zuò, rú guǒ jī huì lái lín, wǒ huì zhuā zhù. wǒ de gōng zuò jīng yàn shǐ wǒ shì hé zhè fèn gōng zuò. bìng qiě wǒ xiàng xìn wǒ néng chéng gōng. wǒ jué dé zì jǐ shì gè gōng zuò qín fèn, fù zé, néng gàn, ér qiě wài xiàng de rén.

Good afternoon, my name is Li Xiaolong. It is really a great honor to have this opportunity to introduce myself. I would like to answer whatever questions you may raise, and I hope I can make a good impression today. I'm thirty years old, born in Beijing. I currently work as a department manager in a trading company. I'm hard-working, responsible, capable, and outgoing. I have lots of interests, such as singing, dancing, drawing, and so on. With my qualifications and experience, I feel I am capable of managing projects I undertake with responsibility and diligence. Your organization could benefit from my analytical and interpersonal skills. I am hoping to get an offer of a better position. If an opportunity knocks, I will take it. My work experience should qualify me for this particular job. I am sure I will be successful.

At the end of this chapter, we will introduce you to Chinese zodaics, including 鼠（shǔ）, 牛（niú）, 虎（hǔ）, 兔（tù）, 龙（lóng）, 蛇（shé）, 马（mǎ）, 羊（yáng）, 猴（hóu）, 鸡（jī）, 狗（gǒu）, and 猪（zhū）. The origin of Chinese zodaics, in fact, has many different versions. If you can use Chinese zodiac to introduce yourself, you listener will be impressed.

Long, long ago, there was no concept of time. There were no clocks or calendars. People wanted to mark the passing of time but didn't know how. Therefore, they sought advice from the Emperor, known for his wisdom in such matters. He pondered for a considerable time before deigning to offer his learned advice: "Because animals and humans have a close affinity and the names of animals are easily remembered, they should be used to symbolize time. Henceforth, a river race shall be held to determine those animals best suited to signify time".

Thereupon the event was held. All manner of beasts attended. The cat and the mouse, who were good friends, discussed the best manner in which to cross, as neither could swim. They decided to ask the ox to aid them. The ox, being a sincere and kindhearted soul, agreed to carry them across. The race began and the ox, who was by far the best swimmer, emerged in the lead. As they neared the finish line, the cat proudly rose and declared the three of them to be the first to cross the line. However, the mouse, a cunning and selfish soul, secretly desired to cross the line first. He caught the cat unaware, pushed him into the water., and jumped behind the ox's ear.

The ox, unaware of the commotion, swam on to the finish line. Just as he reached the shore, the mouse leaped forward and ran to victory, quickly followed by the ox, the tiger, the rabbit, the dragon, the snake, the horse, the sheep, the monkey, the rooster, the dog, and the pig.

The exhausted cat finally scrambled to shore, but the race was already over. The cat was extremely angry at the mouse, and every time they met, the cat would try to bite him. He then told of the mouse's crime to all his progeny, beginning a feud between the two animals which continues to this very day.

The mouse, knowing full-well his sin, skulked away in guilt and spent the rest of his days hiding in dark, sullen places.

The rabbit, who could not swim, made the crossing by leaping across the other animal's heads. He acquired his peculiarly shaped mouth because he ran too fast, and after crossing the finish line, ran into a tree.

The dragon, who should have been placed higher in the ranking, had been busy in the heavens creating thunder and lightning. He absent-mindedly made the thunder too loud, which caused minor deafness. As a consequence, he did not hear the start of the race and had to come from behind to acquire fifth place.

The snake, in order to defeat the horse, scared him and dashed in front. Unfortunately for his, he ran too fast, causing his four legs to break off, leaving him in his present legless state.

The sheep, monkey, and rooster had agreed to make the crossing together. They did so by putting the sheep on the shoulders of the monkey, who in turn sat upon the back of the rooster. As they were crossing, the sheep who was a sort of lookout saw the dog who was naughtily bathing in the river and scolded him severely. The dog continued the race and finished next to last but didn't really care. The sheep ended up overstraining his eyes and permanently damaged his vision. The monkey, who sat far too long, acquired a permanently red posterior. The rooster, who had been supporting the group, lost two of his original four legs as they were crushed.

The pig finished last as he decided to finish eating before crossing the river. When he finally made it across, he entreated the Emperor for more food. His gluttony caused him to become the laughing stock of all those present.

This is a story about how the system of Chinese zodiacs was created. In China, each year is denoted by one of twelve different animals. Your zodiac is supposed to be an indicator of your personality.

In addition, more and more Chinese people, especially the younger generation, have started to believe in astrology. During your self-introduction, you can also talk about that. Here are the expressions of constellations in Chinese.

白羊座（bái yáng zuò）Aries

金牛座（jīn niú zuò）Taurus

双子座（shuāng zǐ zuò）Gemini

巨蟹座（jù xiè zuò）Cancer

狮子座（shī zi zuò）Leo

处女座（chù nǚ zuò）Virgo

天平座（tiān píng zuò）Libra

天蝎座（tiān xiē zuò）Scorpio

射手座（shè shǒu zuò）Sagittarius

摩羯座（mó jié zuò）Capricorn
水瓶座（shuǐ píng zuò）Aquarius
双鱼座（shuāng yú zuò）Pisces

Chapter 10: Formulating Questions and Dialogue:

As we learned in Chapter 7, there are five different kind of questions: the yes or no question, the question using an interrogative pronoun, the affirmative and negative question, the alternative question, and the rhetorical question. Now, let's learn how to form these questions.

Yes or no questions are formed by adding the interrogative particle 吗 (ma) or 吧 (ba) at the end of a declarative sentence. For example:

她是张教授（tā shì zhāng jiào shòu）。

She's Professor Zhang.
她是张教授吗（tā shì zhāng jiào shòu ma）？
Is she Professor Zhang?
他明天回来（tā míng tiān huí lai）。
He will be back tomorrow.
他明天回来吧（tā míng tiān huí lai ba）？
Will he be back tomorrow?
Questions using interrogative pronouns are made from declarative sentences by replacing the enquired information with the

interrogative pronoun. What should be specially noted is that the word order of such a question is exactly the same as that of the declarative sentence, i.e. the question is formed by putting the interrogative pronoun in the position where the answer is expected, not at the beginning. For example:
那是我的外套（nà shì wǒ de wài tào）。
That is my coat.
那是谁的外套（nà shì shuí de wài tào）？
Whose coat is that?
餐馆在路的左侧（cān guǎn zài lù de zuǒ cè）。
The restaurant is on the left side of the road.
餐馆在哪里（cān guǎn zài nǎ lǐ）？
Where is the restaurant?
For more interrogative pronouns, you can review our previous chapters.
好吗/行吗/可以吗/对吗（hǎo ma/xíng ma/kě yǐ ma/duì ma）can be used at the end of declarative sentence to form affirmative and negative questions. For example:
我们听听音乐，好吗（wǒ men tīng tīng yīn yuè, hǎo ma）？
Let's listen to the music, shall we?
这个单词这么念，对吗（zhè gè dān cí zhè me niàn, duì ma）？
This word is pronounced like this, right?
Another way to form affirmative and negative questions is by putting affirmative and negative forms of the predicate together. For example:
好不好（hǎo bú hǎo）
行不行（xíng bù xíng）
能不能（néng bù néng）
对不对（duì bú duì）
是不是（shì bú shì）
你能不能帮帮我（nǐ néng bù néng bāng bāng wǒ）？
Can you help me or not?
我是不是在做梦（wǒ shì bú shì zài zuò mèng）？

Am I dreaming or not?

The alternative question is a question in which several alternatives are paralleled by the conjunction 还是（hái shì）for the answerer to choose. The basic patterns are:

是（shì）……还是（hái shì）……?

Sometimes the first 是（shì）can be ommited. For example:

她是美国人还是法国人（tā shì měi guó rén hái shì fǎ guó rén）?
Is she American or a French?

他高还是你高（tā gāo hái shì nǐ gāo）?
Which one of you is taller? You or him?

Rhetorical questions are often formed by two major patterns:

Using 哪儿……啊 to refute a certain case that is not in keeping with the fact and using 不是……吗 to express the meaning of certainty. For example:

我哪儿知道啊（wǒ nǎr zhī dào a）?
I don't really know.

你哪儿不知道啊（nǐ nǎr bù zhī dào ā）?
How can you not know?

你不是去过我家吗（nǐ bú shì qù guò wǒ jiā ma）?
You have been to my house, haven't you?

不是你去过我家吗（bú shì nǐ qù guò wǒ jiā ma）?
Wern't you the one that was at my house.

Before we more on, let's learn to make the question more polite.

Pattern: 请问 (qǐng wèn) + question

A question prefaced with 请问 (qǐng wèn) is much more polite than one that is not. The English translation of 请问 (qǐng wèn) depends on the context.

Example:

请问这个多少钱 (qǐng wèn zhè gè duō shǎo qián)?
May I ask how much this is?

请问书店在哪里 (qǐng wèn shū diàn zài nǎ lǐ)?
Could you please tell me where the bookstore is?

Buying and Ordering

How do I ask "Do you have any…"?

Pattern: 有没有（yǒu méi yǒu）+ the thing you are looking for

This pattern is used for asking if someone has something, whether or not something is available, or even whether or not something exists.

Examples:

有没有塑料袋（yǒu méi yǒu sù liào dài）?
 Do you have any plastic bags?

有没有现金（yǒu méi yǒu xiàn jīn）?
Do you have any cash?

How do I ask "How much do/does… cost"?

Pattern: the thing you are interested in + 多少钱（duō shǎo qián）

Examples:

纪念品多少钱（jì niàn pǐn duō shǎo qián）?
How much do souvenirs cost?

火车票多少钱（huǒ chē piào duō shǎo qián）?
How much does the train ticket cost?

How do I ask to buy something of a certain cost?

This pattern is complicated, but worth learning if you need to buy items denominated by price:

我要（wǒ yào）+ number of items + measure word + cost + 的（de）+ item

For example:

我要两个十块钱的杯子（wǒ yào liǎng gè shí kuài qián de bēi zi）。
I want two 10 *yuan* cups.

我要买六支三元的笔（wǒ yào mǎi liù zhī sān yuán de bǐ）。
I want to buy six 3 *yuan* pens.

How do I say "I'm a bit hungry（thirsty, sleepy, etc.）"?

Pattern: subject + 有点（yǒu diǎn）+ adjective

For example:

我有点饿（wǒ yǒu diǎn è）。
I'm a bit hungry.

我有点渴（wǒ yǒu diǎn kě）。
I'm a bit thirsty.
这里有点冷（zhè lǐ yǒu diǎn lěng）。
It's a little cold here.
How do I say "a sweet one（a big one, a shiny one, etc.）"?
Pattern: adjective + 的（de）
我要那个大的（wǒ yào nà gè dà de）。
I want that big one.
他喜欢咸的（tā xǐ huān xián de）。
He likes the salty kind.
你想吃甜的吗（nǐ xiǎng chī tián de ma）?
Do you want to have something sweet?
How do I ask an either/or question?
Pattern: A + 还是（hái shì）+ B
For example:
For adjectives:
这是酸的还是辣的（zhè shì suān de hái shì là de）?
Is this sour or hot?
你要大的还是小的（nǐ yào dà de hái shì xiǎo de）?
Do you want a big one or a small one?
For nouns:
你想喝可乐还是啤酒（nǐ xiǎng hē kě lè hái shì pí jiǔ）?
Do you want to have a bottle coke or some beer?
How can I compare two things?
Pattern: A + 比（bǐ）+ B + adjective
For example:
这件比那件贵（zhè jiàn bǐ nà jiàn guì）。
This one is more expensive than that one.
这个比那个好吃(zhè gè bǐ nà gè hǎo chī)。
This thing tastes better than that.
Another way to compare is by using 一点（yì diǎn）. Pattern: adjective + 一点（yì diǎn）

For example:

这件外套便宜一点（zhè jiàn wài tào pián yi yì diǎn）。
This coat is a little cheaper.

这家店的价格高一点（zhè jiā diàn de jià gé gāo yì diǎn）。
The price of this store is a little higher.

How do I place an order at a restaurant or store?

Pattern: subject + 要（yào）+ amount + measure word + item

For example:

我要两碗面（wǒ yào liǎng wǎn miàn）。
I'll have two bowls of noodles.

我要这件外套（wǒ yào zhè jiàn wài tào）。
I want this coat.

How do I say what color of something I want?

Pattern: color + 的（de）or color + 色（sè）+ 的（de）

Example:

我要那个红的（wǒ yào nà gè hóng de）。
I want that red one.

我想买那个白色的（wǒ xiǎng mǎi nà gè bái sè de）。
I want to buy that white colored one.

Can you buy or order things in Chinese now? If you are still wondering how, let's read these dialogues together!

Dialogue 1:

A: 你要买什么（nǐ yào mǎi shén me）？
What would you like to buy?

B: 我想看看那件T恤（wǒ xiǎng kàn kan nà jiàn T xù）。
I would like to look at that T-shirt.

A: 你要什么颜色（nǐ yào shén me yán sè）？
What color do you want?

B: 我要那个白的（wǒ yào nà gè bái de）。
I want that white one.

A: 给你这件（gěi nǐ zhè jiàn）。
Please take a look at this one.

B: 这件太小了。有大号的吗（zhè jiàn tài xiǎo le. yǒu dà hào de ma）？
This one is too small, do you have a bigger size?
A: 对不起，白色没有大号的了，你试试这件蓝色的吧（duì bù qǐ, bái sè méi yǒu dà hào de le, nǐ shì shi zhè jiàn lán sè de ba）。
Sorry, we don't have a bigger size of the white one. Please try this blue one.
B: 很漂亮，我买了。多少钱（hěn piào liang, wǒ mǎi le. duō shǎo qián）？
It's beautiful. I'll take it. How much?
A: 200块（liǎng bǎi kuài）。
200 yuan.

Dialogue 2:
A: 你饿了吗（nǐ è le ma）？
Are you hungry?
B: 有点儿（yǒu diǎn er）。
A little.
A: 我们出去吃饭吧（wǒ men chū qù chī fàn ba）。
Let's go out to eat.
A: 请给我菜单，我要点菜（qǐng gěi wǒ cài dān, wǒ yào diǎn cài）。
Please give me a menu. I'd like to order.
C: 您想吃点什么（nín xiǎng chī diǎn shén me）？
What would you like to eat?
A: 你有什么好建议（nǐ yǒu shén me hǎo jiàn yì）？
Any good suggestion?
C: 这里的清蒸鱼很好，来两份试试吧（zhè lǐ de qīng zhēng yú hěn hǎo, lái liǎng fèn shì shi ba）。
Our steamed fish is very good. Would you lke to have a try?
A: 好，那就来两盘（hǎo, nà jiù lái liǎng pán）。
Sure. Two dishes of steamed fish then.
C: 好的。喝点什么（hǎo de. hē diǎn shén me）？
Ok. What would you like to drink?

A: 我要一瓶啤酒（wǒ yào yì píng pí jiǔ）。
I would like to have a bottle of beer.

B: 一杯红酒（yì bēi hóng jiǔ）。
A glass of wine.

C: 请等一下，菜马上就来（qǐng děng yí xià, cài mǎ shàng jiù lái）。
Please wait a moment. The dishes will be served soon.

B: 买单（mǎi dān）。
Check please.

C: 好的。一共九十五块。您给我一百块，找您三块零钱（hǎo de. yí gòng jiǔ shí wǔ kuài. nín gěi wǒ yì bǎi kuài, zhǎo nín sān kuài líng qián）。
Ok. The total is 97 *yuan*. You gave me 100 *yuan*. Here it is your change, 3 *yuan*.

B: 请给我发票（qǐng gěi wǒ fā piào）。
May I have a receipt?

C: 没问题。欢迎下次光临（méi wèn tí. huān yíng xià cì guāng lín）。
No problem. Please come again soon.

At Work/School/College

How do I ask "What does... mean"?
Pattern: unfamiliar word + 是（shì）+ 什么意思（shén me yì sī）
Examples:
这句话是什么意思 (zhè jù huà shì shén me yì sī)？
What does this sentence mean?

How do I ask how to do something?
Pattern: subject + 怎么（zěn me）+ verb
For example:
传真机怎么用（chuán zhēn jī zěn me yòng）？
How do I use the fax machine?
这道题怎么做（zhè dào tí zěn me zuò）？

How do I solve this question?
How do I say I want to do something myself?
The sentence pattern is often used when emphasizing that one can or will do something themselves and doesn't need assistance. Pattern: pronoun + 自己（zì jǐ）+ verb

For example:
我自己来（wǒ zì jǐ lái）。
I'll do it myself.
我自己去（wǒ zì jǐ qù）。
I can go there myself.
他自己没问题（tā zì jǐ méi wèn tí）。
He can do that by himself.
How do I say "I want to do something"?
Pattern: subject + 想（xiǎng）+ verb + object

For example:
我想请个假（wǒ xiǎng qǐng gè jià）。
I want to take a day off.
你想休息一下吗（nǐ xiǎng xiū xī yī xià ma）?
Do you want to take a break?
How do I ask "Do you have…"?
Chinese often uses a topic-comment sentence pattern during work, and this pattern can be used to ask the "Do you have…" question.
Pattern: topic + 有没有（yǒu méi yǒu）

For example:
工作服有没有（gōng zuò fú yǒu méi yǒu）?
Do you have work clothes?
安全帽有没有（ān quán mào yǒu méi yǒu）?
Do you have a safety helmet?
How do I politely ask someone to do something for me?
Pattern: 请（qǐng）+ 你（nǐ）+ 帮（bāng）+ who + do what

For example:
请帮我开门（qǐng bāng wǒ kāi mén）。
Please open the door for me

请你帮我修理打印机（qǐng nǐ bāng wǒ xiū lǐ dǎ yìn jī）。
Please fix the printer for me.

请你帮我向老师请假（qǐng nǐ bāng wǒ xiàng lǎo shī qǐng jià）。
Please help me ask for leave from the teacher

How do I say "wait a minute (a moment, a bit, etc.)"

Pattern: verb + 一下（yí xià）

For example:

等一下（děng yí xià）wait a minute

看一下（kàn yí xià）look for a moment

让一下（ràng yí xià）move a bit

How can I politely make a request?

Pattern: 麻烦（má fan）+ 你/您（nǐ/nín）+ request

For example:

麻烦你给我那个本子（má fan nǐ gěi wǒ nà gè běn zi）。
Can I trouble you to give me that notebook?

麻烦你帮我写份报告（má fan nǐ bāng wǒ xiě fèn bào gào）。
Can I trouble you to write me a report?

麻烦您到我公司来一趟（má fan nín dào wǒ gōng sī lái yí tàng）。
Can I trouble you to come over to our company?

How do I state a time?

For hours, use this pattern: number + 点（diǎn）

Adding 钟（zhōng）after 点（diǎn）is optional in this pattern. For example:

三点（sān diǎn）three o'clock

四点钟（sì diǎn zhōng）four o'clock

For minutes, use the pattern : number + 分（fēn）

For example:

三点十分（sān diǎn shí fēn）2:10

四点五十三分（sì diǎn wǔ shí sān fēn）4:53

How do I say "I am doing something"?

Pattern: 在（zài）+ verb

For example:

我在打电话（wǒ zài dǎ diàn huà）。
I'm on the phone.
他在听音乐（tā zài tīng yīn yuè）。
He's listening to music.

What is the word order for using 已经（yǐ jīng）in a sentence?

Pattern: subject + 已经（yǐ jīng）+ predicate

For example:
他已经工作两年（tā yǐ jīng gōng zuò liǎng nián）。
He has been working for two years already.
你已经在厕所很久（nǐ yǐ jīng zài cè suǒ hěn jiǔ）。
You've already been in the bathroom a long time!

Notice that, unlike "already" in English, 已经（yǐ jīng）can't be placed at the end of a sentence.

How do I make a suggestion?

One pattern for making suggestions is: noun phrase/sentence + 怎么样（zěn me yàng）

For example:
先写报告怎么样（xiān xiě bào gào zěn me yàng）？
How about we write the report first?
去打篮球怎么样（qù dǎ lán qiú zěn me yàng）？
What about playing basketball?

Another way to make a suggestion is with the particle 吧 (ba).

For example:
我们走吧（wǒ men zǒu ba）。
Let's leave.
我们去开会吧（wǒ men qù kāi huì ba）。
Let's go to the meeting.

How do I say "Did you do something or not"?

Pattern: subject + 有没有（yǒu méi yǒu）+ verb + object

For example:
你有没有带工作证（nǐ yǒu méi yǒu dài gōng zuò zhèng）？
Did you bring your work card or not?

你有没有关上教室的窗户（nǐ yǒu méi yǒu guān shàng jiào shì de chuāng hu）？
Did you close the window of the classroom?
The answer to this question is really easy, just simply repeat the verb with 了（le）at the end for a positive answer; or say 没（méi）at first and then repeat the verb for a negative answer.
How do I say "before/after doing something…"?
Pattern: verb + noun + 以后/以前（yǐ hòu/yǐ qián）
放学以后我们去打篮球吧（fàng xué yǐ hòu wǒ men qù dǎ lán qiú ba）？
Let's play basketball after school.
上班之前我去了趟医院（shàng bān zhī qián wǒ qù le tàng yī yuàn）。
I went the hospital before going to work.
What is the sentence pattern for making an appointment including time and place?
Pattern: subject + time + place + predicate
For example:
我们三点在广场见（wǒ men sān diǎn zài guǎng chǎng jiàn）。
Let's meet at the plaza at three.
我一会儿去机场接你（wǒ yì huìr qù jī chǎng jiē nǐ）。
I'll pick you at the airport later.
Here are more sentences you may find useful when you speak Chinese in real life:
对不起，我迟到了（duì bù qǐ, wǒ chí dào le）。
Sorry, I'm late.
这个字/词怎么读（zhè gè zì/cí zěn me dú）？
How do you pronounce this character/word?
请您再说一遍（qǐng nín zài shuō yí biàn）。
Please say it again.
请您慢一点（qǐng nín màn yì diǎn）。
Please speak a little slowly.

这是我的名片（zhè shì wǒ de míng piàn）。
Here's my business card.

我来这里开会（wǒ lái zhè lǐ kāi huì）。
I'm here for a meeting.

我们可以定个见面时间吗（wǒ men kě yǐ dìng ge jiàn miàn shí jiān ma）？
May I make an appointment?

Travelling

China has an excellent rail network which links all the major cities and smaller towns, as well as an extensive bus system for long-distance travel. Most big cities have their own underground subway systems as well as taxis and public buses. Although you can rent a car in many cities, you can usually only drive within the city limits, and may have to hire a driver if you wish to travel farther around this vast country.

How do I ask "Where can I…"
Pattern: 哪里（nǎ lǐ）+ 可以（kě yǐ）+ verb + object
For example:
哪里可以吃饭（nǎ lǐ kě yǐ chī fàn）？
Where can we get something to eat?
哪里可以打车（nǎ lǐ kě yǐ dǎ chē）？
Where can I take a taxi?

How do I state a destination?
Pattern: 到（dào）+ place
For example:
到火车站（dào huǒ chē zhàn）。
To the train station.
到机场（dào jī chǎng）。
To the airport.

How do I say "the car, the train, or whatever to somewhere"?
Pattern: 到（dào）+ destination + possessive
到上海的火车在哪里（dào shàng hǎi de huǒ chē zài nǎ lǐ）？

Where is the train to Shanghai?

出租车不到喜来登酒店吗（chū zū chē bú dào xǐ lái dēng jiǔ diàn ma）？

Is this cab to Sheraton Hotel?

How do I ask "Where is…"?

Pattern: place + 在哪里（zài nǎ lǐ）

For example:

飞机场在哪里（fēi jī chǎng zài nǎ lǐ）？

Where is the airport?

厕所在哪里（cè suǒ zài nǎ lǐ）？

Where is the bathroom?

What is the answer to "Where is..."?

Pattern: destination + 在（zài）+ direction or direction + 有（yǒu）+ place

For example:

火车站在前面（huǒ chē zhàn zài qián miàn）。

The train station is ahead.

那边有公园（nà biān yǒu gōng yuán）。

There is park over there.

How do I answer "how long" questions?

Below are sample answer patterns for "how long" questions like

你已经在中国多久（nǐ yǐ jīng zài zhōng guó duō jiǔ）？

How long have you been in China?

一分钟（yì fēn zhōng）。

One minute.

For this pattern, you must add 钟（zhōng）

一个小时（yí gè xiǎo shí）。

One hour.

一天（yì tiān）。

A day.

一个星期（yí gè xīng qī）。

A week.

一个月（yí gè yuè）。

A month.

一年（yì nián）。

One year.

Note which of the above phrases require a measure word and which do not.

How do I say that doing something is (not) permitted somewhere?

Pattern: place + 可以/不可以（kě yǐ/bù kě yǐ）+ action

For example:

这里可以停车（zhè lǐ kě yǐ tíng chē）。

It's permitted to stop the vehicle here.

在博物馆不可以吸烟（zài bó wù guǎn bù kě yǐ xī yān）。

You are not allowed to smoke in the museum.

Notice in Chinese word order that the place comes first.

Here are more sentences you may find useful when you speak Chinese in real life:

书店怎么去（shū diàn zěn me qù）？

How do I get to the bookstone?

我迷路了（wǒ mí lù le）。

I'm lost.

附近有厕所吗（fù jìn yǒu cè suǒ ma）？

Is there a toilet nearby?

最近的酒店有多远（zuì jìn de jiǔ diàn yǒu duō yuǎn）？

How far is the nearest hotel?

这是去公园的路吗（zhè shì qù gōng yuán de lù ma）？

Is this the road to the park?

我上车之前要检票吗（wǒ shàng chē zhī qián yào jiǎn piào ma）？

Do I stamp the ticket before boarding?

从哪个站台离开（cóng nǎ gè zhàn tái lí kāi）？

Which platform does it leave from?

需要多长时间（xū yào duō cháng shí jiān）？

How long does it take?

我在哪能找到出租车（wǒ zài nǎ néng zhǎo dào chū zū chē）?
Where can I get a taxi?
你能把我放在这里吗（nǐ néng bǎ wǒ fàng zài zhè lǐ ma）?
Can you drop me here?
我能要一个收据吗（wǒ néng yào yí gè shōu jù ma）?
May I have a receipt?
我去哪办理登记手续（wǒ qù nǎ bàn lǐ dēng jì shǒu xù）?
Where do I check in?
我需要办理一件行李托运（wǒ xū yào bàn lǐ yí jiàn xíng li tuō yùn）。
I'm checking in one suitcase.
我什么时候登机（wǒ shén me shí hòu dēng jī）?
What time do I board?
我找不到我的行李（wǒ zhǎo bú dào wǒ de xíng li）。
I can't find my luggage.

Other things you may want to know

Unlike in America, most Chinese doctors are based in hopitals; you will need to make an appointment to see one. Many pharmacies stock Western medicines as well as traditional Chinese remedies and can treat you for most minor health problems. It is a good idea to familiarize yourself with a few basic phrases for use in an emergency or in case you need to visit a pharmacy or doctor.
What is the sentence pattern for saying some part of my body hurts?
Pattern: 我（wǒ） + part of body + problem
For example:
我头疼（wǒ tóu téng）。
I have a headache.
我背酸（wǒ bèi suān）。
I have a sore back.
我眼睛不舒服（wǒ yǎn jīng bù shū fú）。
My eyes are uncomfortable.
我耳朵很痒（wǒ ěr duǒ hěn yǎng）。

My ear is itchy.

Other useful sentences:

我有健康保险（wǒ yǒu jiàn kāng bǎo xiǎn）。
I have health insurance.

我需要看牙医（wǒ xū yào kàn yá yī）。
I need a dentist.

治咳嗽该吃什么药（zhì ké sòu gāi chī shén me yào）？
What can I take for coughs?

有副作用吗（yǒu fù zuò yòng ma）？
Are there side effects?

我需要一个处方吗（wǒ xū yào yí gè chù fāng ma）？
Do I need a prescription?

In the event of an emergency, you should dial one of the following emergency numbers: 110 for the police, 119 for the fire department, and 120 for an ambulance. If you are the victim of a crime or you've lost your passport and money, you should report the incident to the police, although it may be best to seek advice first from your local embassy or consulate staff. Here are some useful sentences:

救命（jiù mìng）！
Help!

放手（fàng shǒu）！
Let go.

打电话报警（dǎ diàn huà bào jǐng）！
Call the police!

有人受伤了，请快来（yǒu rén shòu shāng le, qǐng kuài lái）！
Someone's injured, please come quickly!

我孩子丢了（wǒ hái zi diū le）。
My child is missing.

我被打劫了（wǒ bèi dǎ jié le）。
I've been robbed.

Common conversation starters:

你家里有几口人（nǐ jiā lǐ yǒu jǐ kǒu rén）？
How many people are there in your family?

你有没有兄弟姐妹（nǐ yǒu méi yǒu xiōng dì jiě mèi）？
Do you have any brothers or sisters?
你结婚了吗（nǐ jié hūn le ma）？
Are you married?
你有孩子吗（nǐ yǒu hái zi ma）？
Do you have any children?
你的老家在哪里（nǐ de lǎo jiā zài nǎ lǐ）？
Where is your hometown?
你一个月多少钱（nǐ yí gè yuè duō shǎo qián）？
How much do you make a month?
你的工资多少钱（nǐ de gōng zī duō shǎo qián）？
What is your salary?
你想家吗（nǐ xiǎng jiā ma）？
Do you miss your home?
你在这里习惯吗（nǐ zài zhè lǐ xí guàn ma）？
Are you accustomed to life here?
你觉得这里怎么样（nǐ jué de zhè lǐ zěn me yàng）？
What do you think about here?

APPENDIX: VOCABULARY
Glossary of Nouns

姓（xìng）surname
名（míng）first name
姓名（xìng míng）full name
爸爸（bà ba）dad
父亲（fù qin）father
妈妈（mā ma）mom
母亲（mǔ qin）mother
叔叔（shū shu）uncle
阿姨（ā yí）aunt
爷爷（yé ye）grandfather (father's dad)
奶奶（nǎi nai）grandmother (father's mom)
外公（wài gōng）grandfather (mother's dad)
外婆（wài pó）grandmother (mother's mom)
女儿（nǔ er）daughter
儿子（ér zi）son
先生（xiān shēng）Mr., sir
女士（nǔ shì）Madam, Miss., Ms.
夫人（fū rén）Ms.
太太（tài tài）Ms.

哥哥（gē ge）older brother
姐姐（jiě jie）order sister
弟弟（dì di）younger brother
妹妹（mèi mei）younger sister
男孩（nán hái）boy
女孩（nǚ hái）girl
朋友（péng yǒu）friend
室友（shì yǒu）roommate
同学（tóng xué）classmate
伙伴（huǒ bàn）companion
恋人（liàn rén）lover
伴侣（bàn lǚ）mate, partner
夫妻（fū qī）husband and wife
丈夫（zhàng fu）husband
老公（lǎo gōng）husband
妻子（qī zǐ）wife
老婆（lǎo pó）wife
医生（yī shēng）doctor
经理（jīng lǐ）manager
演员（yǎn yuán）actor, actress
歌手（gē shǒu）singer
记者（jì zhě）journalist
工程师（gōng chéng shī）engineer
顾问（gù wèn）consultant
老师（lǎo shī）teacher
警察（jǐng chá）police officer
工人（gōng rén）worker
司机（sī jī）driver
公务员（gōng wù yuán）government official
律师（lǜ shī）lawyer

科学家（kē xué jiā）scientist
服务员（fú wù yuán）waiter, waitress
接待员（jiē dài yuán）receptionist
厨师（chú shī）chef
翻译（fān yì）translator
作家（zuò jiā）writer
艺术家（yì shù jiā）artist
销售员（xiāo shòu yuán）salesperson
商人（shāng rén）businessman, businesswoman
企业家（qǐ yè jiā）enterpreneur
学生（xué shēng）student
秘书（mì shū）secretary
护士（hù shì）nurse
消防员（xiāo fáng yuán）firefighter
飞行员（fēi háng yuán）pilot
空乘（kōng chéng）flight attendant
教授（jiāo shòu）professor
校长（xiào zhǎng）headmaster
志愿者（zhì yuàn zhě）volunteer
军人（jūn rén）armyman
文化（wén huà）culture
语言（yǔ yán）language
文学（wén xué）literature
历史（lì shǐ）history
法律（fǎ lǜ）law
经济（jīng jì）economy
数学（shù xué）math
化学（huà xué）chemistry
物理（wù lǐ）physics
生物（shēng wù）biology

政治（zhèng zhì）politics
地理（dì lǐ）geography
外语（wài yǔ）foreign language
哲学（zhé xué）philosophy
心理学（xīn lǐ xué）psychology
国家（guó jiā）country
中国（zhōng guó）China
中国人（zhōng guó rén）Chinese
英国（yīng guó）Britain
美国（měi guó）America
加拿大（jiā ná dà）Canada
德国（dé guó）Germany
法国（fǎ guó）France
意大利（yì dà lì）Italy
日本（rì běn）Japan
俄罗斯（é luó sī）Russia
韩国（hán guó）South Korea
澳大利亚（ào dà lì yà）Australia
新西兰（xīn xī lán）New Zealand
丹麦（dān mài）Denmark
荷兰（hé lán）Holland
挪威（nuó wēi）Norway
瑞典（ruì diǎn）Sweden
瑞士（ruì shì）Switzerland
西班牙（xī bān yá）Spain
葡萄牙（pú táo yá）Portugal
希腊（xī là）Greece
土耳其（tǔ ěr qí）Turkey
伊朗（yī lǎng）Iran
伊拉克（yī lā kè）Iraq

巴西（bā xī）Brazil

阿根廷（ā gēn tíng）Argentina

泰国（tài guó）Thailand

菲律宾（fēi lǜ bīn）the Philippines

新加坡（xīn jiā pō）Singapore

马来西亚（mǎ lái xī yà）Malaysia

印度尼西亚（yìn dù ní xī yà）Indonesia

肯尼亚（kěn ní yà）Kenya

埃及（āi jí）Egypt

坦桑尼亚（tǎn sāng ní yà）Tanzania

南非（nán fēi）South Africa

印度（yìn dù）India

巴基斯坦（bā jī sī tǎn）Pakistan

斯里兰卡（sī lǐ lán kǎ）Sri Lanka

时间（shí jiān）time

生日（shēng rì）birthday

年（nián）year

月（yuè）month

星期（xīng qī）week

周（zhōu）week

日（rì）day

天（tiān）day

前天（qián tiān）the day before yesterday

昨天（zuó tiān）yesterday

今天（jīn tiān）today

明天（míng tiān）tomorrow

后天（hòu tiān）the day after tomorrow

周末（zhōu mò）weekend

时候（shí hòu）time

现在（xiàn zài）present, now

早晨（zǎo chén）morning

中午（zhōng wǔ）noon

下午（xià wǔ）afternoon

晚上（wǎn shàng）evening, night

一会儿（yī huìr）a little while

好久（hǎo jiǔ）for a long time

小时（xiǎo shí）hour

分钟（fèn zhōng）minute

秒（miǎo）second

地方（dì fang）place

免税店（miǎn shuì diàn）duty-free shop

学校（xué xiào）school

公园（gōng yuán）park

游乐园（yóu lè yuán）amusement park

动物园（dòng wù yuán）zoo

电影院（diàn yǐng yuàn）cinema, movie theater

图书馆（tú shū guǎn）library

广场（guǎng chǎng）square, plaza

银行（yín háng）bank

医院（yī yuàn）hospital

诊所（zhěn suǒ）clinic

机场（jī chǎng）airport

邮局（yóu jú）post office

火车站（huǒ chē zhàn）train station

汽车站（qì chē zhàn）bus station

码头（mǎ tóu）dock

酒店（jiǔ diàn）hotel

餐馆（cān guǎn）restaurant

咖啡馆（kā fēi guǎn）coffee house

茶楼（chá lóu）tea house

警察局（jǐng chá jú）police office
监狱（jiān yù）jail
商店（shāng diàn）store
市场（shì chǎng）market
超市（chāo shì）supermarket
夜总会（yè zǒng huì）nightclub
酒吧（jiǔ ba）bar
音乐会（yīn yuè huì）concert
大学（dà xué）university
书店（shū diàn）bookstore
花店（huā diàn）florist
百货商店（bǎi huò shāng diàn）department store
首饰店（shǒu shì diàn）jewelry store
服装店（fú zhuāng diàn）boutique
五金店（wǔ jīn diàn）hardware store
纪念品店（jì niàn pǐn diàn）souvenir shop
面包房（miàn bāo fáng）bakery
蛋糕店（dàn gāo diàn）cake shop
停车场（tíng chē chǎng）parking lot
加油站（jiā yóu zhàn）gas station
市政厅（shì zhèng tīng）town hall
博物馆（bó wù guǎn）museum
艺术馆（yì shù guǎn）art gallery
星巴克（xīng bā kè）Starbucks
肯德基（kěn dé jī）KFC
麦当劳（mài dāng láo）McDonalds
汉堡王（hàn bǎo wáng）Burger King
米其林（mǐ qí lín）Michelin
必胜客（bì shèng kè）Pizza Hut
喜来登酒店（xǐ lái dēng jiǔ diàn）Sharaton Hotel

希尔顿酒店（xī ěr dùn jiǔ diàn）Hilton Hotel
香格里拉酒店（xiāng gé lǐ lā jiǔ diàn）Shangri-la Hotel
公司（gōng sī）company
工厂（gōng chǎng）factory
车间（chē jiān）workshop
办公室（bàn gōng shì）office
天安门广场（tiān ān mén guǎng chǎng）Tiananmen Square
故宫（gù gōng）Forbidden City
长城（cháng chéng）Great Wall
钱（qián）money
现金（xiàn jīn）cash
零钱（líng qián）change
发票（fā piào）invoice
汇率（huì lǜ）exchange rate
取款机（qǔ kuǎn jī）cash machine
信用卡（xìn yòng kǎ）credit card
人民币（rén mín bì）Chinese *yuan*
美金（měi jīn）US dollar
港币（gǎng bì）Hong Kong dollar
日元（rì yuán）yen
英镑（yīng bàng）pound
欧元（ōu yuán）euro
护照（hù zhào）passport
飞机（fēi jī）airplane
出租车（chū zū chē）taxi
自行车（zì xíng chē）bike
摩托车（mó tuo chē）motor bike
火车（huǒ chē）train
救护车（jiù hù chē）ambulance
消防车（xiāo fáng chē）fire engine

警车（jǐng chē）police car
卡车（kǎ chē）truck
餐车（cān chē）dining car
列车卧铺（liè chē wò pù）sleeper car
地铁（dì tiě）subway
公交车（gōng jiāo chē）bus
船（chuán）boat
渡轮（dù lún）ferry
游艇（yóu tǐng）yacht
直升机（zhí shēng jī）helicopter, chopper
车顶行李架（chē dǐng háng lǐ jià）roofrack
儿童座椅（ér tóng zuò yǐ）child seat
行李箱（xíng lǐ xiāng）trunk
轮胎（lún tāi）tire
发动机（fā dòng jī）engine
站台（zhàn tái）platform
航站楼（háng zhàn lóu）terminal
柜台（counter）guì tái
交通信号灯（jiāo tōng xìn hào dēng）traffic light
人行道（rén xíng dào）pedestrian crossing
票（piào）ticket
登机牌（dēng jī pái）boarding pass
自动售票机（zì dòng shòu piào jī）automatic ticket machine
救生衣（jiù shēng yī）life jacket
救生圈（jiù shēng quān）life ring
公路（gōng lù）road
高速公路（gāo sù gōng lù）highway
铁轨（tiě guǐ）rail
收费站（shōu fèi zhàn）toll gate
东边（dōng biān）east

西边（xī biān）west
南边（nán biān）south
北边（běi biān）north
上面（shàng mian）above
下面（xià mian）under
左边（zuǒ biān）left
右边（yòu biān）right
旁边（páng biān）next to
对面（duì miàn）opposite
前面（qián mian）ahead, in front
后面（hòu mian）at the back, behind
里面（lǐ mian）inside
外面（wài mian）outside
路口（lù kǒu）crossing
啤酒（pí jiǔ）beer
红酒（hóng jiǔ）wine
水（shuǐ）water
茶（chá）tea
果汁（guǒ zhī）juice
咖啡（kā fēi）coffee
卡布奇诺（kǎ bù qí nuò）cappuccino
拿铁（ná tiě）latte
可乐（kě lè）coke
雪碧（xuě bì）sprite
芬达（fēn dá）fanta
苏打水（sū dǎ shuǐ）soda
威士忌（wēi shì jì）whisky
白兰地（bái lán dì）brandy
鸡尾酒（jī wěi jiǔ）cocktail
朗姆（lǎng mǔ）rum

白酒（bái jiǔ）white wine
热巧克力（rè qiǎo kè lì）hot chocolate
酸奶（suān nǎi）yogurt
牛奶（niú nǎi）milk
豆奶（dòu nǎi）soy milk
汤（tāng）soup
水果（shuǐ guǒ）fruit
苹果（píng guǒ）apple
香蕉（xiāng jiāo）banana
桔子（jú zi）orange
芒果（máng guǒ）mango
葡萄（pú tao）grape
木瓜（mù guā）papaya
西瓜（xī guā）watermelon
梨（lí）pear
柠檬（níng méng）lemon
青柠（qīng níng）lime
梅子（méi zi）plum
樱桃（yīng tao）cherry
番石榴（fān shí liu）guava
草莓（cǎo méi）strawberry
菠萝（bō luó）pineapple
荔枝（lì zhī）lychee
椰子（yē zi）coconut
桃（táo）peach
枣（zǎo）date
石榴（shí liu）pomegranate
火龙果（huǒ lóng guǒ）pitaya
蔬菜（shū cài）vegetable
茄子（qié zi）eggplant

生菜（shēng cài）lettuce
土豆（tǔ dòu）potato
胡萝卜（hú luó bo）carrot
洋葱（yáng cōng）onion
韭菜（jiǔ cài）leek
黄瓜（huáng guā）cucumber
西红柿（xī hóng shì）tomato
芹菜（qín cài）celery
西兰花（xī lán huā）broccoli
玉米（yù mǐ）corn
大白菜（dà bái cài）cabbage
莴笋（wō sǔn）asparagus
青椒（qīng jiāo）green pepper
海带（hǎi dài）seaweed
葱（cōng）green onion
姜（jiāng）ginger
蒜（suàn）garlic
菜单（cài dān）menu
早饭（zǎo fàn）breakfast
午饭（wǔ fàn）lunch
晚饭（wǎn fàn）dinner
零食（líng shí）snack
鸡蛋（jī dàn）egg
肉（ròu）meat
鸡（jī）chicken
鹅（é）goose
鱼（yú）fish
鸭（yā）duck
猫（māo）cat
狗（gǒu）dog

鹿（lù）deer
驴（lǘ）donkey
猴（hóu）monkey
海鲜（hǎi xiān）sea food
牛肉（niú ròu）beef
螃蟹（páng xiè）crab
牛排（niú pái）steak
虾（xiā）shrimp
猪肉（zhū ròu）pork
鱿鱼（yóu yú）squid
羊肉（yáng ròu）mutton
糖（táng）sugar
盐（yán）salt
醋（cù）vinegar
酱油（jiàng yóu）soy sauce
胡椒（hú jiāo）pepper
面包（miàn bāo）bread
果酱（guǒ jiàng）jam
奶油（nǎi yóu）cream
奶酪（nǎi lào）cheese
黄油（huáng yóu）butter
香肠（xiāng cháng）sausage
米饭（mǐ fàn）cooked rice
馄饨（hún tun）wontons
饺子（jiǎo zi）dumplings
包子（bāo zi）steamed dumplings
面条（miàn tiáo）noodles
月饼（yuè bǐng）mooncake
汉堡（hàn bǎo）hamburger
热狗（rè gǒu）hot dog

薯条（shǔ tiáo）French fries
炸鸡（zhá jī）fried chicken
三明治（sān míng zhì）sandwich
橄榄（gǎn lǎn）olive
坚果（jiān guǒ）nut
虾片（xiā piàn）prawn cracker
沙拉（shā lā）salad
爆米花（bào mǐ huā）popcorn
甜点（tián diǎn）dessert
冰淇淋（bīng qí lín）ice cream
棒棒糖（bàng bang táng）lolipop
果冻（guǒ dòng）jelly
蛋糕（dàn gāo）cake
衣服（yī fú）clothes
裤子（kù zi）pants
牛仔裤（niú zǎi kù）jeans
T恤（T xù）t-shirt
衬衫（chèn shān）shirt
毛衣（máo yī）sweater
大衣（dà yī）coat
裙子（qún zi）skirt, dress
西装（xī zhuāng）suit
夹克（jiá kè）jacket
背心（bèi xīn）vest
短裤（duǎn kù）shorts
领带（lǐng dài）tie
帽子（mào zi）hat, cap
鞋子（xié zi）shoes
靴子（xuē zi）boots
皮鞋（pí xié）leather shoes

运动鞋（yùn dòng xié）sneakers
高跟鞋（gāo gēn xié）high heels
凉鞋（liáng xié）sandals
人字拖（rén zì tuō）flip-flops
袜子（wà zǐ）socks
内衣（nèi yī）underwear
内裤（nèi kù）panties
项链（xiàng liàn）necklace
手链（shǒu liàn）bracelet
手表（shǒu biǎo）watch
戒指（jiè zhǐ）ring
耳钉（ěr dìng）earring
泳装（yǒng zhuāng）swimsuit
墨镜（mò jìng）sunglasses
遮阳帽（zhē yáng mào）sun hat
眼（yǎn）eye
耳（ěr）ear
口（kǒu）mouth
嘴（zuǐ）mouth
舌头（shé tou）tongue
喉咙（hóu long）throat
鼻（bí）nose
身体（shēn tǐ）body
头（tóu）head
脸（liǎn）face
头发（tóu fa）hair
脖子（bó zi）neck
手臂（shǒu bì）arm
手（shǒu）hand
指甲（zhǐ jia）nail

手腕（shǒu wàn）wrist
肩（jiān）shoulder
胸（xiōng）chest
腹（fù）belly
腿（tuǐ）leg
膝盖（xī gài）knee
脚（jiǎo）foot
脚踝（jiǎo huái）ankle
中药（zhōng yào）traditional Chinese medicine
西药（xī yào）Western medicine
绷带（bēng dài）bandage
创可贴（chuàng kě tiē）adhesive bandage
胶囊（jiāo náng）capsule
药片（yào piàn）pill
吸入器（xī rù qì）inhaler
栓剂（shuān jì）suppository
滴剂（dī jì）drop
喷雾器（pēn wù qì）spray
糖浆（táng jiāng）syrup
软膏（ruǎn gāo）ointment
足球（zú qiú）football
护腕（hù wàn）wristbands
乒乓球（pīng pāng qiú）ping pong
乒乓球拍（pīng pāng qiú pāi）table tennis bat
网球（wǎng qiú）tennis
网球拍（wǎng qiú pāi）tennis racket
高尔夫球（gāo ěr fū qiú）golf
高尔夫球杆（gāo ěr fū qiú gān）golf club
羽毛球（yǔ máo qiú）badminton
篮球（lán qiú）basketball

排球（pái qiú）volleyball
体操（tǐ cāo）gymnastics
武术（wǔ shù）martial art, kung fu
跆拳道（tái quán dào）taekwondo
房子（fáng zi）house
楼（lóu）building
电梯（diàn tī）elevator
家（jiā）home
门（mén）door
房间（fáng jiān）room
房间号（fáng jiān hào）room number
日用品（rì yòng pǐn）articles for daily use
口红（kǒu hóng）lipstick
香水（xiāng shuǐ）perfume
筷子（kuài zi）chopstick
刀子（dāo zi）knife
叉子（chā zi）fork
勺子（sháo zi）spoon
餐巾（cān jīn）napkin
纸巾（zhǐ jīn）tissue
盘子（pán zi）plate
碗（wǎn）bowl
杯子（bēi zi）cup
酒杯（jiǔ bēi）glass
词典（cí diǎn）dictionary
名片（míng piàn）business card
便签（biàn qiān）note pad
公文包（gōng wén bāo）briefcase
打印机（dǎ yìn jī）printer
传真机（chuán zhēn jī）fax machine

锁（suǒ）lock

伞（sǎn）umbrella

圆珠笔（yuán zhū bǐ）gel pen

颜色（yán sè）color

礼物（lǐ wù）gift

箱子（xiāng zǐ）case

小冰箱（xiǎo bīng xiāng）min bar

衣橱（yī chú）wardrobe

茶几（chá jǐ）tea table

沙发（shā fā）sofa

椅子（yǐ zǐ）chair

餐桌（cān zhuō）dining table

床（chuáng）bed

被子（bèi zi）quilt

枕头（zhěn tóu）pillow

毯子（tǎn zi）blanket

灯泡（dēng pào）light bulb

插头转换器（chā tóu zhuǎn huàn qì）adapter

电水壶（diàn shuǐ hú）kettle

散热器（sàn rè qì）radiator

挂衣架（guà yī jià）hanger

遥控器（yáo kòng qì）remote control

窗帘（chuāng lián）blind

浴缸（yù gāng）bathtub

肥皂（féi zào）soap

毛巾（máo jīn）towel

浴袍（yù páo）robe

沐浴乳（mù yù rǔ）shower gel

牙膏（yá gāo）toothpaste

牙刷（yá shuā）toothbrash

润肤露（rùn fū lù）body lotion
漱口水（shù kǒu shuǐ）mouthwash
剃须刀（tì xū dāo）razor
剃须泡沫（tì xū pào mù）shaving foam
吹风机（chuī fēng jī）hairdryer
洗发水（xǐ fà shuǐ）shampoo
护发素（hù fà sù）conditioner
指甲刀（zhǐ jiǎ dāo）nail clipper
指甲剪（zhǐ jiǎ jiǎn）nail scissor
梳子（shū zi）comb
风扇（fēng shàn）fan
空调（kōng tiáo）air-conditioner
微波炉（wēi bō lú）microwave
熨斗（yùn dòu）iron
熨衣板（yùn yī bǎn）ironing board
拖把（tuō bǎ）mop
水桶（shuǐ tǒng）bucket
洗衣机（xǐ yī jī）washing machine
冰箱（bīng xiāng）refrigerator
垃圾桶（lā jī tǒng）garbage can
锁（suǒ）lock
钥匙（yào shi）key
烟雾报警器（yān wù bào jǐng qì）smoke alarm
灭火器（miè huǒ qì）fire extinguisher
开瓶器（kāi píng qì）bottle opener
案板（àn bǎn）cutting board
菜刀（cài dāo）kitchen knife
削皮刀（xiāo pí dāo）peeler
打蛋器（dǎ dàn qì）whisk
煎锅（jiān guō）frying pan

砂锅（shā guō）casserole dish
搅拌器（jiǎo bàn qì）blender
烤盘（kǎo pán）cookie sheet
烤箱手套（kǎo xiāng shǒu tào）oven mitts
围裙（wéi qún）apron
推车（tuī chē）grocery cart
篮子（lán zi）basket
打火机（dǎ huǒ jī）lighter
香烟（xiāng yān）cigarette
雪茄（xuě jiā）cigar
烟灰缸（yān huī gāng）ashtray
相机（xiàng jī）camera
相册（xiàng cè）photo album
键盘（jiàn pán）keyboard
鼠标（shǔ biāo）mouse
路由器（lù yóu qì）router
无线网络（wú xiàn wǎng luò）WIFI
密码（mì mǎ）password
书（shū）book
纸（zhǐ）paper
笔（bǐ）pen
铅笔（qiān bǐ）pencil
本子（běn zi）notebook
东西（dōng xi）thing
跨包（kuà bāo）purse
背包（bèi bāo）bag
钱包（qián bāo）wallet
天然气（tiān rán qì）natural gas
电（diàn）electricity
电话（diàn huà）telephone

号码（hào mǎ）number
手机（shǒu jī）mobile
电视（diàn shì）television
电脑（diàn nǎo）computer
笔记本电脑（bǐ jì běn diàn nǎo）lap top
口香糖（kǒu xiāng táng）gum
杂志（zá zhì）magazine
报纸（bào zhǐ）newspaper
小说（xiǎo shuō）novel
漫画（màn huà）comic book
电影（diàn yǐng）movie

Glossary of Verbs

是（shì）to be
有（yǒu）to have
做（zuò）to do
会（huì）can, could, will, would, shall, should
说（shuō）to speak, to say
要（yào）to take, to want, will, would
去（qù）to go
看（kàn）to see, to look at
知道（zhī dào）to know
带（dài）to take, to bring
想（xiǎng）to want, to miss
来（lái）to come
给（gěi）to give
成（chéng）to become, to be done
用（yòng）to use
找（zhǎo）to find
告诉（gào sù）to tell
求（qiú）to beg

埋（mái）to bury
讲（jiǎng）to tell, to speak
离开（lí kāi）to leave
需要（xū yào）to require, to need
工作（gōng zuò）to work
感觉（gǎn jué）to feel
问（wèn）to ask
展示（zhǎn shì）to show
试（shì）to try
叫（jiào）to shout, to call
提供（tí gòng）to offer, to provide
保持（bǎo chí）to keep
拿（ná）to take
转（zhuǎn）to turn
跟（gēn）to follow
喜欢（xǐ huān）to like
帮（bāng）to help
跑（pǎo）to run
走（zǒu）to walk
写（xiě）to write
动（dòng）to move
玩（wán）to play
付（fù）to pay
听（tīng）to listen
相信（xiàng xìn）to believe
允许（yǔn xǔ）to allow
遇见（yù jiàn）to meet
住（zhù）to live
站（zhàn）to stand
发生（fā shēng）to happen, to take place

拉（lā）to pull
推（tuī）to push
说话（shuō huà）to speak
出现（chū xiàn）to appear
生产（shēng chǎn）to produce
考虑（kǎo lǜ）to consider
建议（jiàn yì）to suggest
期望（qī wàng）to expect
让（ràng）to let
喊（hǎn）to shout
丢（diū）to lose
加（jiā）to add
改变（gǎi biàn）to change
记（jì）to note, to write
买（mǎi）to buy, to purchase
卖（mài）to sell
录（lù）to record
送（sòng）to deliver, to give (as a present)
收（shōu）to collect
决定（jué dìng）to decide
赢（yíng）to win
明白（míng bái）to understand
发展（fā zhǎn）to develop
描述（miáo shù）to describe
同意（tóng yì）to agree
开（kāi）to open, to drive
关（guān）to close
到（dào）to arrive, to reach
建（jiàn）to build
还（huán）to return

画（huà）to draw
希望（xī wàng）to wish, to hope
创造（chuàng zào）to create
等（děng）to wait
造成（zào chéng）to cause
通过（tōng guò）to pass
撒谎（sā huǎng）to lie
接受（jiē shòu）to accept
举（jǔ）to raise, to lift
申请（shēn qǐng）to apply
打（dǎ）to hit, to punch
学习（xué xí）to learn
解释（jiě shì）to explain
借（jiè）to borrow
成长（chéng zhǎng）to grow
上报（shàng bào）to report
宣布（xuān bù）to announce
支持（zhī chí）to support
切（qiē）to cut
形成（xíng chéng）to form
呆（dāi）to stay
减少（jiǎn shǎo）to reduce, to decrease
建立（jiàn lì）to establish
加入（jiā rù）to join
寻求（xún qiú）to seek
实现（shí xiàn）to realize
选择（xuǎn zé）to choose
面对（miàn duì）to face
供应（gōng yīng）to supply
终结（zhōng jié）to end

生（shēng）to give birth
驾驶（jià shǐ）to drive
代表（dài biǎo）to represent
讨论（tǎo lùn）to discuss
放置（fàng zhì）to place
爱（ài）to love
捡（jiǎn）to pick spmething up from the ground
证明（zhèng míng）to prove
穿（chuān）to wear
争吵（zhēng chǎo）to argue
抓（zhuā）to seize, to grasp
欣赏（xīn shǎng）to enjoy
介绍（jiè shào）to introduce
吃（chī）to eat
进（jìn）to enter
退（tuì）to retreat, to move back
出席（chū xí）to attend
指（zhǐ）to point
计划（jì huá）to plan
演（yǎn）to act
影响（yǐng xiǎng）to influence
管理（guǎn lǐ）to manage
识别（shí bié）to identify
谢（xiè）to thank
比较（bǐ jiào）to compare
忘（wàng）to forget
暗示（àn shì）to indicate
加强（jiā qiáng）to strengthen
遭受（zāo shòu）to suffer
出版（chū bǎn）to publish

表达（biǎo dá）to express
躲避（duǒ bì）to avoid, to dodge
完成（wán chéng）to complete, to finish
节省（jiē shěng）to save
设计（shè jì）to design
对待（duì dài）to treat
分享（fēn xiǎng）to share
控制（kòng zhì）to control
移除（yí chú）to remove
拜访（bài fǎng）to visit
扔（rēng）to throw
存在（cún zài）to exist
鼓励（gǔ lì）to encourage
强迫（qiáng pò）to force
反映（fǎn yìng）to reflect
笑（xiào）to smile
哭（kū）to cry
承认（chéng rèn）to admit
假设（jiǎ shè）to assume
代替（dài tì）to replace
准备（zhǔn bèi）to prepare
提高（tí gāo）to improve
填（tián）to fill
提及（tí jí）to mention
打架（dǎ jià）to fight
拒绝（jù jué）to refuse
阻止（zǔ zhǐ）to prevent
教（jiāo）to teach
躺（tǎng）to lie down
揭示（jiē shì）to reveal

陈述（chén shù）to state
操作（cāo zuò）to operate
回答（huí dá）to answer
记录（jì lù）to record
检查（jiǎn chá）to check
释放（shì fàng）to release
延长（yán cháng）to extend
修（xiū）to fix
飞（fēi）to fly
摇（yáo）to shake
签（qiān）to sign
保护（bǎo hù）to protect
适应（shì yìng）to get used to
确认（què rèn）to confirm
协调（xié tiáo）to coordinate
嫁（jià）to marry (female to male)
娶（qǔ）to marry (male to female)
照顾（zhào gù）to take care of
收集（shōu jí）to collect
雇（gù）to hire, to employ
标（biāo）to mark
否认（fǒu rèn）to deny
射（shè）to shoot
瞄准（miáo zhǔn）to aim at
任命（rèn mìng）to appoint
订（dìng）to order
观察（guān chá）to observe
喝（hē）to drink
忽略（hū luè）to ignore
安排（ān pái）to arrange

关注（guān zhù）to focus
尝（cháng）to taste

www.ingramcontent.com/pod-product-compliance
Lightning Source LLC
Chambersburg PA
CBHW070048230426
43661CB00005B/808